MW01106388

PRAISE Fⵁⵔ ⵁⵍⵜⵜⵉⵏⵁ ⵜⵁ 4ⵁ

"*Getting to 40* is a reminder that there is no wealth like knowledge and no poverty like ignorance."
— **Archimedes**

"A book of great insight *Getting to 40* is, for those who value learning, and avoiding the dark side."
— **Yoda**

"The wisdom of R~I~P~P~L~E~S is that it helps us to better understand life, ourselves and the world around us. If you grasp only this concept, *Getting to 40* will be worth your time and investment."
— **Socrates**

"*Getting to 40* reinforces that a career that you enjoy is what puts perfection in your work."
— **Aristotle**

"Mr. Geib has found the elegance in simple equations to explain some very complex topics. I congratulate him."
— **Einstein**

"*Getting to 40* establishes an excellent model for those who believe financial independence is the only path to true freedom."
— **Copernicus**

* Perhaps the voices of wisdom if they were alive today.

Published by BookLocker.com, Inc.,

Bradenton, Florida.

Printed in the United States of America

on acid-free paper.

Booklocker.com, Inc. 2015 First Edition

Cover design by Brandon Geib

Set in Baskerville and DIN

Designed by Brandon Geib

FOR MY PARENTS
SKIP & GINNY

Douglas G. Geib II
MBA & CPA

~

GETTING
TO 40

~

Career Management
and Other
Financial Insights
For My Family

PROLOGUE

To My Sons,

It hardly seems six years since I published my first book, *Getting to 30, Financial Advice for My Three Sons.* As you recall, the objective of that book was to provide you, and the youth of America, a roadmap to financial independence. Today, in an age where financial literacy is finally a buzzword phrase of educators, regulators and even company wellness programs, I am proud to say this book is one of the few that clearly articulates the fundamental financial principles that are key to your future success. More than you know, I appreciate how much each of you have embraced the guiding principles in *Getting to 30.* In many ways, you are so much ahead of your peers when it comes to understanding fundamental financial literacy (which is especially satisfying since none of you were business majors in college).

Getting to 40, Career Management and Other Financial Insights For My Children continues my efforts to help you achieve some sense of stability in a volatile and chaotic world. I'm confident if you embrace the advice herein, you will achieve a level of independence that avoids stagnation and keeps you on a course that will help ensure future prosperity.

I hope you and your peers take the time to read this book (and after you're done, go back and reread *Getting to 30*). I know in our digital age attention spans are short, everyone multitasks and there is this intimate instantaneous connection to our smartphones. For a moment, however, slow down and try to absorb the advice herein. As you will see, my views continue to evolve as I recognize the increasing challenges of your generation. Like any good non-fiction book, if you retain one good idea, then the time you invest reading *Getting to 40* will be worth it.

Today I am a writer but in years past I've been an accountant, an auditor, a consultant, an investor, a financial advisor, a coach, a volunteer, a director, a businessman, and an entrepreneur. Some might even call me a philosopher and a lightning rod for somewhat unconventional thinking and ideas. However, the role that is, and always has been, the most gratifying (and the most challenging) is a parent. I am proud to be your father. Without a doubt all of you are your mother's and my greatest achievements.

Socially, I am an outlier. Neither of my parents had college degrees when I entered my freshman year. Nor were my parents people of influence in high society. My parents didn't have the resources to pay for my education. I didn't attend a prestigious private school or even a high school focused on college prep. Moreover, I didn't graduate from an elite private undergraduate college.

In fact, my first two years of college were spent at a public university's branch campus located in the small farming community of Marion, Ohio. Back then you stayed close to home to minimize costs and earn part of your tuition through various part-time jobs. Upon graduation I never packed my bags and moved to more attractive venues in larger cities and larger markets. I spent 20 years with the same company, all in Ohio, most of it in Columbus. What did I have? A splendid recipe of nature and nurture, mixed with a pinch (maybe several pinches) of adversity. I'm not sure how many of my peers would trade their career paths and personal success for mine. I do know there is no one in the world I would

> **Success in your 30s is doing something you love that generates sufficient earnings to live the lifestyle you want.**

swap with. I hope all of you feel the same about your life as you approach 60 years old.

In a way, all of you are also outliers. Sure, you starting a bit closer to the front of the line. But where you start is no guarantee of success. So, part of *Getting to 40* is my story, woven with the benefit of hindsight and sprinkled with advice I figured out on my own as I went along. As I've said before, I am one data point in your life's journey. Filter my thoughts like you should all suggestions and recommendations. My hope is that much of my advice (which is shared by your mother) will endure and it will become part of the values you pass on to your children.

I've been fortunate in many ways, but one of my greatest pleasures is having the opportunity to travel to many parts of the world. This travel has allowed me to observe many different economies as well as the ruins of ancient civilizations. In fact, I may be one of the few individuals in the world who has had the opportunity to visit the fossilized pulverized city of Pompeii in Italy, the Mayan-Toltec ruins of Chichén Itzá in Mexico, the Great Wall that borders Mongolia, the tranquil crater of Mt. Fuji in Japan, the Terracotta warriors of China, the Inca City of Machu Picchu in Peru, the religious temples of Angkor Wat in Cambodia, and the Potala Palace, the historical residence of the Dalai Lama, in Tibet. I've seen the economic situation of the extremely poor as well as the significant wealth of high society.

These expeditions, along with many others, provide me some unique insights and coupled with my years of practical and successful business experience with Ernst & Young LLP ("EY") and FirstCom Corporation (plus the great education from The University of Chicago and The Ohio State University) allow me to view financial matters entirely from a different perspective than the hypothetical world of academia or the ivory towers of credulous politicians. As you know, I am totally unshackled from any possible conflict of interests and therefore it is easy to only let your best interests drive me.

It hardly seems like twenty years since I left my position at EY. For many reasons, it was a great learning experience since it provided me an opportunity to hone my technical expertise in accounting, auditing, tax and corporate finance as well as my overall management skills. To the best of my knowledge, I was the only individual in EY's history that was able to develop skills as an Audit Partner and a Partner in Corporate Finance. These roles provided me the somewhat unique ability to understand how the numbers in a set of historical financial statements were derived but also what the numbers might mean to investors, financiers and other stakeholders.

In late 1996 I made the decision to leave EY for an opportunity to work with a new entrepreneurial venture called FirstCom. FirstCom was a start-up focused on building and operating state of the art fiber optic networks for businesses in Chile, Peru and Colombia. I was the Senior Executive Vice President, Chief Financial Officer and a member of the Board of Directors. In October 1999, FirstCom was Bloomberg's #1 fastest-growing publicly traded company headquartered in the United States. In late 2000 FirstCom was successfully merged into a new public company which became known as AT&T Latin America. FirstCom may have been one of the few emerging market ventures in the 1990s that actually repaid all of its debt and provided many of its long-term equity investors an attractive return when the Company's market value exceeded $4 Billion in early 2000. However, more importantly, FirstCom introduced high speed Internet services to many South American businesses, enhancing their competitiveness in the new digital economy.

However, despite this historical backdrop, my views have evolved thanks to a relentless pursuit of knowledge and insight. Our home is littered with years of article clippings, book highlights and personal notes which provide me a profound perspicacity. These notes, and the books, articles and conversations that inspired them, provide a unique data base of support for many of my ongoing and always evolving thoughts and ideas.

Getting to 40 is going to introduce you to a plethora of new acronyms beginning with R~I~P~P~L~E~S, and including C.O.O.L. T.E.A.M.S. A.R.T. E.C.O. W.T.F. and perhaps the most important, I.C.O.N. You will learn about the Circle of Commerce and the Ring of Happiness. I'm going to introduce you to some new terms such as The Capitalist Hypocrisy, The Illusion of Markets, The Paradox of Peace, Arbitrage Squeeze, The Algorithms of Value and The Agile Advantage. Accelerating your career will be boiled down to a simple mathematical model. You'll see that many financial strategies can be summarized in very basic formulas such as $S = A$. You'll learn the value of replacing PEDs with PELs. You'll also meet C.H.R.I.S., the agile and fuzzy squirrel that replaces the traditional view of feeding a big fat piggy bank.

As you might recall, *Getting to 30* had a primary theme of Become Educated through the ongoing pursuit of K.I.T.E. (Knowledge, Insight, Technique and Experience). *Getting to 40* takes this a step further and recognizes that in the real world you do need to earn a living, for yourself and your family. It will help you answer many questions including: Are you in the best environment to develop the right skills that will form the foundation of a successful career? Can you achieve financial security and professional fulfillment?

Getting to 40 begins with a new template to help you better understand any economic environment and how members within and outside of different communities interact with each other. Economics is valuable, but only if you understand why its concepts matter, how it shapes human interactions and most importantly, how to integrate economics into your everyday decision making. The economic forces that I will discuss impact the success of every individual and every community they are part of and/or actively participate in. I am confident this discussion will spice up and bring relevance to a science most would agree is even more dismal than accounting.

This template will increase the likelihood you will build a career path that matches the warmth of your dreams and passions with the cold reality of the marketplace. As you know, when it comes to finding the best career path you're running out of time to figure it out. Your 30s is the decade where you will have the greatest energy to pursue and achieve an optimal career path. If you wander through the next decade with no sense of direction it will not bode well for your later years.

Getting to 40 discusses five important processes you must follow to continue on your path to financial independence. These five processes are:

1. Understanding R~I~P~P~L~E~S
2. Creating Your Future
3. Learning to Save
4. Investing With Wisdom
5. Managing Risk

Your 20s was a time of experimentation as you began to emerge as adults and young men. It provided you a lot of time to consider many alternative career paths, what type of profile best fits a life partner and whether children may be in your future. It's nice to have so many possibilities in life; but now, well, you need to focus.

The five principles essentially boil down to a ring of success with the icons of Earn, Consume, Save, Invest and Give. A Ring of Happiness that embraces a circle of financial freedom. As you weave the tapestry of your life, each icon should grow brighter as you grow older.

Love, Dad

CONTENTS

UNDERSTANDING
R~I~P~P~L~E~S

INTRODUCING
THE NEW SOCIAL
ECONOMIC FORCES
THAT SHAPE ALL
COMMUNITIES

During the past several years, in my discussions with you and many of your peers, it is clear that members of our society have a poor understanding of basic economics. My concern is this general lack of insight could jeopardize your journey toward financial independence.

Sadly, this lack of insight no longer seems confined to your generation, which might bring you comfort or tremendous fear. Your youth shielded you from any immediate consequences, but the economic calamity of 2008 was the worst our world had seen for almost four generations. Most economists had no idea this crisis was brewing. Their beliefs in efficient capital markets, rational players, financial innovation, self regulation, leverage and Keynesian monetary policy was blown apart by asset bubbles, illiquid markets, counter-party risk, global imbalances and the imperfect calculus of supply and demand. No wonder people call economics the dismal science. However, as you will see, my approach to teaching you economics is entirely different from the traditionalists and their messy chalkboards of shifting x and y axes. Instead, I use the lexicon of everyday language. I believe this change in mindset will benefit you and your peers, the future leaders of this great nation.

As you soon will learn, R~I~P~P~L~E~S is not only a very powerful acronym but a metaphor as well. Imagine for a moment, lazily relaxing on a sandy beach and gazing out at a sea so calm it looks like a flat mirror of glass stretching to the horizon. Within minutes a small wave washes on to the beach, leaving bits of seaweed and foam before the current ebbs back into the ocean. You pick up a shell, drop it into a small pool of water, alone and isolated from the previous high tide. You watch as the smallest of movements send tiny ripples across the pool, before quickly disappearing. You start to wonder, what made that ocean wave brush along the beach, interrupting the tranquil nature of this vast ocean: maybe a distant storm, perhaps far off ships, a school of dolphins or a warm tropical breeze.

As you read this book I want you to constantly think of this very powerful word called ripples. Every action, whether man-made or attributable to nature or the acts of gods, has a ripple. Searching, detecting, identifying, understanding, influencing, anticipating and predicting these ripples is what drives economics. These ripples are the signals (sometimes faint but usually with hindsight the echoes were obvious) that impact the forces that shape all communities. Recognizing each force is not complex, but understanding how the forces relate to each other and how a single ripple might influence multiple forces will be your challenge.

> The Forces that shape EVERY community are:
> **R**esources
> **I**nfrastructure
> **P**olicy
> **P**rice
> **L**eaders
> **E**ducation;
> all of which work together to achieve a goal of
> **S**tability.

These are the forces of R~I~P~P~L~E~S! Think of these forces as providing a bit of a different spin on the traditional view of economics, a new model to fuse the macro with the micro. R~I~P~P~L~E~S is my Economic Theory of Everything. A model that allows you to understand how the Earth and its communities function from a vantage point high above the minutiae that clouds the interactions of everyday living. In my model Price is only one of six powerful forces. My model doesn't search for an optimal or fair price based on shifting supply and demand curves. No, my end game is Stability. Stability that embraces a certain harmony with others is the outcome I seek.

Picture the first six forces on each side of a cube, wrapped in a banner of Stability. And just like a gyroscope relies on spin and gravity to maintain its motion, our Ripples Cube relies on a complementary interaction of these forces to keep a community's compass spinning toward harmony. If R~I~P~P~L~E~S was a game it would have the complexity of Chess, the uncertainty of billiard balls skittering across a pool table and the winner would possess the skills of a master Bridge player.

For example, some people might argue the reason the United States of America has been so successful is because of the depth and breadth of its natural resources, infrastructure that facilitates mobility of people and ideas, policies that emphasize property rights, human dignity, and the rule of law, monetary

R~I~P~P~L~E~S is my Economic Theory of Everything.

guidelines that minimize inflationary price increases, leaders who mentor entrepreneurs, and education that creates a learning environment that enhances innovation and drives productivity. You can easily see how these themes support the pillars of R~I~P~P~L~E~S. However, as you will learn, the actual ripples that drive these Forces in the United States, and in other communities, are much more complex than the reasons listed above.

COMMUNITIES

When you think about a community it is easy to visualize all of the different organizations, groups or social networks that are part of our lives. A community might be a traditional group of people within well-defined national borders of a sovereign country, family members who share certain customs and beliefs, employees who work at a corporation, politicians who oversee governments, athletes who participate on a sports team, and world leaders who meet once a year at the World Economic Forum in Davos, Switzerland. A community might operate within the legal framework of a larger community or it might operate in the vast underworld of illicit and other illegal activities. All of us participate in multiple communities. For example, over the years my communities included work, family, church, schools, sports, charitable endeavors, alumni organizations, homeowners associations, and professional societies as well as larger communities such as the city, county, state and the country where I live. Your list would be different, but just as diverse.

Today, many communities spring up quickly, facilitated by the virtual world of the Internet and social and professional networking sites like Facebook, Reddit, Twitter and LinkedIn. Such communities transcend the visible boundaries that historically restricted members to more traditional communities rooted in physical location. Although virtual communities may dissolve quickly once members accomplish certain objectives, many of these networks actually pursue lifetime hobbies or special interests and therefore cement longer-term relationships.

There are a couple of ways you can become part of a community. You are born into many communities (your family and your country of origin) while others you choose to join. Some communities might draft you (the U.S. military during the Vietnam War), others may appoint you (committees and teams at work), and occasionally you self appoint (you become a parent or a volunteer). However, regardless of how we become part of a community, all of us look to our communities to fulfill certain needs. They might be physical needs (food and shelter), intellectual needs (schools and universities), social needs (friends and caregivers), spiritual needs (religion and morals), emotional needs (happiness and contentment), and financial needs (jobs and careers). Because communities exist to promote a shared vision (or a common cause) an individual will usually give up some freedoms in exchange for their participation in the community. Hopefully such participation also provides a benefit to the individual as well as to the overall community.

Depending on one's view, communities can be "good" or "bad." For example, in January 2002, President Bush (after the horrific attacks of September 11th) tagged Iran, Iraq and North Korea with the moniker "Axis of Evil". And not to be outdone, al Qaeda, the cross border terrorist organization led by Osama bin Laden, labeled the American people as devil worshipers who endorsed the murder of innocent civilians.

From my perspective, **communities move from "good" to "bad" when they take on more cult like characteristics.** That is, when communities begin to control what you do (your behavior); what you read (your access to information); how you think (your opinion on issues); how you feel (your belief of right and wrong); and what you earn and how you spend (your financial freedoms); then such communities descend into the abyss of darkness. Obedience becomes the ideology of the occult. People do what they are ordered to do without a second thought. As you will discover, such shadow societies are much more prevalent than most people imagine.

As an individual, the most significant decision you make every day is how much time to invest in each of your communities. This decision is typically based on those communities you care about the most, those communities where you think you have the greatest impact, and those communities that benefit you personally or professionally. For most individuals their most important community is their immediate family and may include parents, siblings, a spouse and/or children, and often times very close friends. Of course, the amount of attention you might give to your highest priority communities will be driven by its overall stability. That is, if a community of interest is relatively stable you will give it less attention versus the communities you love which appear to be in perpetual upheaval.

Often, people have a desire (and the freedom) to leave a community, but they choose to stay in an environment they hate. Why? Maybe they have a job that would be difficult to replace. Perhaps they bought a home they cannot sell. Sometimes they have relatives (elderly parents) who depend on them. Often they have ties to trusted professionals (doctors, dentists, accountants, lawyers) that require a "high touch" relationship. Many times they are divorced and their children still live in the community. In any event, this lack of mobility traps many people. Individuals who become ensnared (either because they lack freedom and cannot leave or they have freedom but choose to stay) in an environment they want to leave usually develop a loathing toward those who they feel are most responsible for their frustration. This is especially true of the youth; principally because of a fear that all they have to look forward to is years of perpetual misery. Communities where a large number of its members feel trapped, either because they lack basic freedoms or they have few opportunities, will always teeter on the precipice of instability and chaos.

As you grow older, a number of themes will transcend all communities. You will discover members of a community who embrace guiding principles that support a common ideology have the best prospects for a happy and harmonious life. However, you will learn the happiness you chase is sometimes fleeting, existing for one moment and then vanishing the next. You will see the best communities are those where the members have an active involvement and a sincere caring for others. You will witness that the most respected members of a community are those who act like coaches and not prima donna power brokers. You will understand selfishness has its limitations in a global community where there is a certain amount of interdependency among all life forms that inhabit this planet. You will observe the freedom of choice and mobility among members is what truly nurtures the innate power of every community. You will realize prosperity depends on competition, cooperation and compromise. You will marvel how consistent values, common causes, and majestic visions can unite a community into a compelling mission. You will appreciate how the Forces of R~I~P~P~L~E~S must interact in an integrated and symbiotic process to increase the likelihood that a community can achieve and sustain success. **The Forces of R~I~P~P~L~E~S shape every community and your most important communities shape you.**

RESOURCES

Resources are the single most fundamental force that shapes any community. Resources mask themselves in three separate but interrelated domains – Natural (those that evolve from our planet), Human (those that manifest itself in its people) and Money (created by man for the initial purpose of facilitating the trade of natural and human resources). Resources that are managed in a prudent manner will enhance the standard of living and quality of life for members of its community. On the other hand, key resources that are depleted, wasted, destroyed, exploited and otherwise mismanaged will leave most members of a closed community trapped in perpetual misery, dependent on the charity of outsiders.

Natural resources exist simply because we live on this prodigious planet called Earth. These resources are so extensive that it is difficult, some would argue impossible, to identify all of them. For example, Earth's resources include more than 4,500 minerals that have been formed through eons of geological processes. Just think about it, different inorganic minerals, each having specific physical properties and chemical compositions, make up every nonliving product. Or consider the Svalbard Global Seed Vault built by Norway. This vault contains 400,000 seed samples stored in sealed envelopes, tucked away in temperature-controlled rooms on the small island of Spitsbergen, located 810 miles from the North Pole. These seeds are part of the recipe of soil, water and sunlight we mix together to grow the food that nourishes us and many of the other living creatures that roam this planet.

The minerals that compose the things we buy and the seeds that grow the food we eat are both scattered across endless topography that shape the landscape of our communities. Rivers, lakes, oceans, forests, hills, mountains, plains, swamps, sand dunes and other terrain are not only part of, but often form the physical boundaries of many communities. This terrain is influenced by weather patterns (hot, cold, windy, calm, sunlight, cloudy, etc.) as well as geological changes (earthquakes, mudslides, floods, volcanic eruptions, etc.) that create many of the other organic resources contained in the Earth's crust (like oil, coal and natural gas). All of these resources we can visually observe; yet some of the Earth's most important treasures are ones we will never see (gamma rays, x-rays, microwaves, radio waves, etc.). Specifically, hidden from our view is electromagnetic radiation that provides the wireless spectrum that facilitates today's global communication. Even airspace is becoming more important as communities wrestle with how to regulate where drones can fly.

Human resources represent the approximately 7 billion people that occupy our planet in 2015; which is expected to stabilize at around 9 billion people in 2070. In 2015, approximately 84% of the Earth's population are younger than 54 years old; slightly more than 50% live in urban areas; males slightly outnumber females; more than 88% are religious; 84% of those age 15 and over can read and write; and although there are more than 6,900 languages spoken throughout the world more than half of the world's population communicates in Chinese, Arabic, English, Spanish, French, or Russian.

As you know, the Earth's natural resources (including rights of way, ports of entry and other routes of passage) and human resources are not distributed equally throughout our planet. Consequently, there always will be (and there always has been) an equality gap among people (and communities) because the world's resources are not allocated in an equitable way. In other words, the world will never have a "level playing field" among all communities.

Because resources are not evenly distributed throughout the world, people (and their communities) **must trade things they have for things they want.** Humans create (or add value to) most of the things that a community trades; including trading people (slavery) or parts of people (blood, organs, embryos, sperm and genetic codes).

People (and their communities) also decide (or accept) the relative value of the things they trade. It is this difference in relative value that enhances or diminishes the wealth of a community. Money is the metric that is used to measure relative value in the same way that time is used to measure how our day was spent.

In 2015, the estimated amount of money in the world is 70 trillion U.S. dollars: or approximately $10,000 per person. Most of the currency circulating throughout the planet has been created by the governments of the world's largest economies, specifically, the United States, the European Union, China and Japan. In theory, governments create money to manage economies, which often includes the financing of deficit spending designed to promote price stability and employment.

From a global perspective, **money facilitates trade, but it does not represent wealth** mainly because money that is an asset for someone is a liability for someone else. The U.S. Dollar in my pocket is a liability of the United States of America. In other words, if all of the world's economies increased the money supply ten fold, the citizens of the world would not be wealthier.

However, money is more powerful than natural resources and people because money is the grease that lubricates the engine of economic exchange. If the U.S.A. remains a viable and strong economy, then I can use the U.S. Dollar to store value until I decide to trade it for something else. For example, if I buy land with my money I now have tangible wealth; if I acquire education with my money I now have marketable skills. My land and my skills are my assets. **Real wealth does not create a liability for others.** The best way to think of the distribution of global wealth is to imagine a world where there is no money. Then focus solely on the natural and human resources that exist in each community.

It is almost impossible to quantify the Earth's natural resources, calculate the exact number of people on our planet, and determine the amount of money circulating throughout the World. In other words, it is impossible to put a value on the Earth. Imagine for a moment you are the supreme commander of all of Earth, and aliens approached you and wanted to buy Earth. **How would you**, the supreme commander, **value Earth** and what would you take in exchange for payment? The aliens probably would first tell you to exclude the human race from the equation since it would be hard for them to imagine how any intelligent being would design such a screwed up world. With no humans around, the U.S. Dollar no longer has any value and of course you would have no idea how to value any type of alien currency. The point is the relative value we attribute to any of Earth's resources is not only complex (since it is dependent on thousands of variables) but also quite arbitrary.

Communities that consume more than they produce must fund this trade deficit with debt or charitable gifts from others. In theory, on a global scale, trade should balance. That is, the trade deficit of one community should be a trade surplus for another community. However, in practice, global gifts of charity and other forms of "foreign" aid (which include debts that have been forgiven) become the equity plug to the world's money supply. When money becomes decoupled from the global communities' balance sheets, currency is left in the hands of global financial speculators. Often these speculators then become the primary source of funds for troubled, unstable and rogue regimes.

During the next decade the stories you follow will highlight several points of view that may surprise you. The parables will convince you that all communities must trade, or live in fear that the resources they try to protect will be taken, or exploited, by outsiders. You will see those who control the resources are the ones who decide today's winners and losers. It will anger you that the battle over natural resources is never a fair fight. It will bother you that imaginary conflicts that pit public interest against private concerns are nothing but clever ruses to hide the benefits that accrue to people in power. It will enrage you once you realize the wasteful depletion of natural resources will leave nothing for the children of tomorrow. You will watch as new communities erase the traditional importance of physical borders as the endless boundaries of social networks become more relevant. However, you will learn communities that surround themselves by physical barriers will fight even harder to keep the less desirable people out, and to convince the most promising people to stay. You will witness how easily money is used to overheat an economy, and then watch as it melts, burning the dreams of communities who thought they could find salvation in pieces of paper. Yet, the more you read, the better you will understand, why many of today's victors will be tomorrow's failures. And, in the end, you will celebrate once you picture how an improved process of allocating a community's limited resources does, in fact, benefit all of humanity.

INFRASTRUCTURE

Infrastructure is the critical force that connects and adds value to a community's resources. It exists principally to enable transactions among individuals and their communities. These transactions include trade (in both goods and services), the exchange of information and ideas (patents, research and processes), the transport of people (workers, students, tourists, refugees) and the movement of money.

For example, people need safe drinking water and basic food staples to survive and therefore a caring and capable community will build transportation networks that link all of the critical components of its supply chain (the producer, the grower, the processor, the manufacturer, the distributor, the retailer and eventually the consumer). **The more ubiquitous the infrastructure, the greater the velocity of exchange among individuals** (assuming leaders have enacted favorable policies and equitable prices).

Every community must identify its most important resources (natural, human and/or financial) because the harvesting of these resources allows a community to trade what it has for what it needs (and/or what it wants). For example, if the community has a basic natural resource, it might be a producer. If it has access to certain rights of way (rivers, sea lanes, connecting land masses, etc.) it might be a transporter. If it is the gateway to large population groups, it might be a retailer. If it has lots of money, it might be an investor. If it has lots of people, it might provide physical labor and/or intellectual knowledge. No one piece of the supply chain is more important to a community's wealth versus another. However, the ability to build the best infrastructure to leverage a community's natural talents is what eventually spreads prosperity among its citizens.

In addition to identifying its most important resources, a community needs to project how these resources will change in the future. For example, are the communities' natural resources renewable (water, wind, sunlight, land, etc.) or finite (mineral deposits like gold, silver, copper, uranium, etc.)? In theory, infrastructure that is built to capitalize on renewable resources will generally have an infinite life (a windmill), as long as such infrastructure is maintained and updated. On the other hand, infrastructure that supports natural resources that eventually will be depleted only needs to survive the useful life of the resource (a railway needs to outlast the coal that it hauls).

Many communities will have some limitations to the infrastructure it can develop. Rugged terrain increases the costs for roads, railways and pipelines. Land-locked communities must secure rights of way from neighbors. Risks of natural disasters limit desirability of certain locations. Frozen tundra is difficult to develop. Such constraints, coupled with volatile political systems and other man made disasters, make it difficult, sometimes impossible, to attract necessary infrastructure financing. **Resources have minimal worth if infrastructure cannot be built to facilitate trade and monetize value.**

This risk of building infrastructure that is not needed or not building infrastructure that is needed is further complicated by one additional, but extremely critical variable. Neighbors! That is, should we cooperate or compete with our neighbors based on an assessment of risks/rewards and costs/benefits. Do we duplicate, or complement? Communities, of course, have different needs and objectives. Trains, trucks and automobiles travel through different communities; airplanes fly in and out of different locations, oil and natural gas move through pipelines that often connect the source in one community with a user in another. Often members of a community understand the value of infrastructure, but an attitude of "not in my backyard" permeates their decision making.

As you can see, determining the depth and breadth of infrastructure development is one of the most difficult questions for any community. Is it better to let infrastructure respond to growth and the needs of the community or should a community make significant investments in infrastructure in the belief that growth follows? Is it better to take the risk that a project might be unsound and never justify the investment risk or better to battle traffic jams and similar clogs in a supply chain? Should the environment stay pristine even if it means opportunities for a better standard of living may never accrue to members of other communities?

A community relationship with its trading partners (and their relationships with others in the world) along with evolving demographics, trends in technology, improvements in productivity, shifting alliances among major stakeholders, and geographic challenges due to natural disasters and changes in weather patterns puts a terrific strain on decisions involving infrastructure. However, the benefits of getting the infrastructure question right and the consequences of getting it wrong have a tremendous impact on whether a community can improve the standard of living of its members.

Communities that deplete their natural resources (or had minimal natural resources to begin with) have a greater need to develop the skills of their people. Human resources can be in the form of physical labor or intellectual capital. The trade of physical labor tends to piggyback on the infrastructure that is used to transport products and goods (roads, freeways, airports, rail, etc.). The trade of intellectual capital relies principally on infrastructure that facilitates human communication. In today's world, the most critical infrastructure that supports communication is commonly known as the Internet. As communities grow and become more diverse and more complex, it is human communication up, down and throughout the supply chain that makes trade, especially with respect to financial services, more efficient and effective.

Relative to the infrastructure we use today to transport people, products and ideas, the infrastructure we use to store, inventory and move money is relatively modest. Unlike natural resources that are confined to their physical location and people who for various reasons stay within the physical boundaries of their communities, money is essentially ubiquitous (except, in those rare situations, where the flow of money has been restricted by a community). In fact, a community's "money" is nothing more than a digitized number that shows up on a bank statement with a currency sign. In other words, money is not demarcated by any physical boundaries. In a manner of seconds it can zip around the world, flowing to the people (and/or the entities they represent) who control the resources. Communities that run out of money do so because (a) they have no natural resources left to trade for money, (b) they have no services that their citizens can provide to others, (c) they waste their savings on frivolous items or risky ventures, or (d) they have other problems (which we will discuss later) that give rise to political and economic uncertainty. In other words, there is nothing these communities can provide that others want.

Infrastructure can facilitate trade that is positive or negative for a community. Drug cartels (trading cocaine, heroin, methamphetamine and marijuana) and other illicit activities use the same infrastructure that enable legitimate transactions as well as their own transportation and production centers. In addition, when wars break out between communities critical infrastructure (pipelines, airports, ports, etc.) is targeted for destruction early in the campaigns.

In addition to physical or political barriers, money will always be a constraint when it comes to building infrastructure. Infrastructure will always be a community's biggest investment and like all investments it must be paid for in one form or the other. Regardless of whether infrastructure is funded from public or private channels, communities only have a limited amount of sources to pay for this investment, which include the following:

- Trading some of their resources
- Assessing a charge to those who benefit (a toll)
- Levying a tax to all members of the community (a tax)
- Bundling the costs with a related good or service (a fee)

When such fees are not sufficient to pay for the investment over its estimated useful life (because of cost overruns, shoddy construction, natural catastrophes or dismal estimates of projected demand) then constituents are assessed higher fees in the future and/or investors accept a lower return (including loss of principal) because of the asset's impairment. In addition, when sources are no longer sufficient to maintain existing infrastructure, then obsolescence will eventually slow the velocity and efficiency of trade and the exchange of resources.

Bad infrastructure investments are probably the number one cause of permanent increases in the world's money supply. Bad investments lead to bad loans and whether through government bailouts (direct repayment to the investors or subsidizing the fees of its constituents) or cash that flows to the traders of debt and equity instruments, a greater percentage of the world's money supply ends up in the hands of financial speculators.

As you follow tomorrow's headlines you will see why infrastructure is such a strong force in a community's quest for happiness. You will begin to believe trade is the best way to redistribute wealth and reallocate power and why infrastructure is such a powerful tool to help ordinary citizens prosper. You will see that the right infrastructure project can be the community anchor that connects members to a network that enables their success. You will appreciate it when a community has the foresight to maintain its infrastructure today, so it continues to provide value tomorrow. It will sadden you when you learn many communities refuse to develop the necessary infrastructure that would help their people escape poverty. It will disturb you when you see how the lack of investment in the right infrastructure traps a community in mediocrity and poverty. It will bother you when you witness communities who become dependent on others for resources, simply because they choose not to (or cannot) develop the infrastructure that would provide them something to trade. It will anger you when you watch communities build useless infrastructure, solely to keep people working today, knowing that resources are being exhausted and leaving little behind for the necessary jobs of the future. It will frustrate you when projects that enhance a community today, slowly destroy the environment its citizens will depend on for survival tomorrow. However, upon reflection, you will recognize how much more prosperous a community will be if its infrastructure is the catalyst that marries its resources with the needs and desires of the people.

POLICY

Rules, principles and values reflect the policies that influence the behavior of members of a community. Every community is governed by laws and regulations. Policies often are reduced to specific written rules but policy can function effectively, and often does, when rules are communicated through rituals, stories and other forms of audio and visual stimulation.

For example, one of the most famous set of written rules, at least for the religious communities of Christianity, Judaism, and Islam, are the scriptures God embossed on two stone tablets. God gave these plaques to Moses on top of an Arabian Mountain called Mount Sinai. These rules, famously documented as the Ten Commandments in the

Bible's Old Testament and referred to in various sections of the Qur'an, are moral imperatives that God directed his followers to obey. Written rules, of course, have no meaning to those who can't read. Nevertheless, billions of religious souls (some of whom are illiterate) are still aware of such rules because the community that nurtures them ensures such proclamations are part of their upbringing.

Policies exist for a number of different reasons. The most important policies keep people safe, protect our environment, help us stay healthy, educate our youth, and protect our property (our land, our home, our money, etc.). Communities also create a framework of rules in the hope that trade flows more efficiently. Consequently, it is relatively easy for people who govern to rationalize new policy, or changes in existing policies, because of these relatively broad mandates.

It is easy for most of us to rationalize policies that benefit us (or people that we love or support) are "good" policies. On the other hand, policies that are not in our best interests we usually deem as "bad." A good policy is always "fair" (moral, ethical and just) to those who support the policy and "unfair" (immoral, unethical and not just) to those who do not support the policy. Because new policies will always benefit some citizens at the expense of someone, the challenge, and the rolling controversy, is whether the benefit exceeds the harm.

Policies can be made by a few individuals in positions of authority like dictators (e.g. parents or teachers), plutocrats (e.g. owners of a company), and oligarchs (e.g. the board of directors of a charity) or by many individuals who work to achieve a consensus (e.g. student teams working on class projects, members of a homeowners association, representatives elected to the U.S. Congress, etc.). It's crucial for you to understand how policies evolve and how rules reflect such policies. It is this insight that may allow you to begin a process to change the policies you do not like. This understanding is especially critical in communities where you are a permanent or long-term member.

Members of a community may not respect a community's policies and therefore may choose not to follow its rules. There are numerous reasons for such disobedience. People might deem the policies unfair or in conflict with beliefs they embrace from other communities. Maybe the benefit of cheating outweighs the cost of compliance. Perhaps they are not aware of the rules that they violate. It could be the community does not enforce its rules and therefore there is minimal risk of getting caught. Certainly it's conceivable that community members break rules because they are stupid and lack common sense. Of course, it is always possible individuals who do not follow the rules may be mentally ill and sadly they have a warped sense of reality since their brains are wired irrationally. Often, policies aren't blatantly violated but instead individuals aggressively pursue loopholes that are inconsistent with the spirit of the laws. Sometimes the most responsible people of a community circumvent the rules and the most reckless people abide by them.

In any event, the number of policies (and the corresponding rules that support a community's policies) will always increase as populations within a broad community become more heterogeneous and interdependent competing communities become more complex. Moreover, there will always be an increase in the number of rules when the responsible leaders of a community believe others in the community behave irresponsibly (mainly because the leaders now have to define what is responsible behavior). **When people trust and understand each other there is minimal need for rules that define the appropriate behaviors of a community.** Stable communities tend to have more members who trust each other and generally comply with the rules. Unstable communities have levels of distrust among members and therefore continually battle issues of noncompliance. Like all R~I~P~P~L~E forces there is an optimal point in the model where there is the right balance with respect to the number of rules, coupled with a reasonable level of compliance, where diverse populations actually can (and do) live together in relative harmony.

ENVIRONMENT

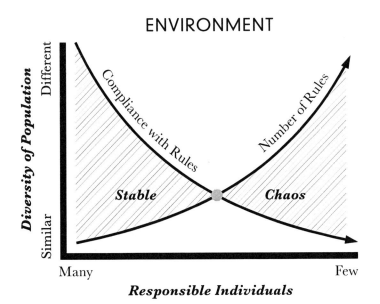

Responsible members of a community will follow its policies if they believe most, if not all members, do the same. Responsible members tend to support policies when the rules are:

- Clear and concise
- Fair to a large number of groups within a community
- Enforced in a timely and equitable way

When a large percentage of community members circumvent the rules using the tools of impunity, conflicts of interests, influence-peddling and other forms of corruption, then a community essentially becomes lawless and policies no longer matter. **Responsible behavior cannot survive if irresponsible behavior is allowed to thrive** (if for no other reason that the responsible people will eventually leave the community).

Most federal, state and local policies we follow were implemented by past rulers. Especially in the United States a plethora of rules, layered on top of an increasing level of complexity, dictate appropriate behavior. In a community that requires consensus for action, it is virtually impossible to undo legislation from years of ineptitude, which makes it increasingly difficult to craft coherent policies in the future. Moreover, many laws which may have made sense in the past are no longer applicable in today's environment. As this complexity increases, the velocity of trade slows as citizens spend more time complying with convoluted laws or circumventing barriers that complicate decision making.

Perhaps not surprising, in a relative sense, the quality of life is always going to be more miserable for those people who do not want to live within the boundaries of the rules that leaders enact for their communities. Moreover, if members of a community fail to self regulate, then the community will tend to enact more policies or else it will slip into a quagmire of lawlessness.

As you listen to tomorrow's headlines you will agree policies that expand the velocity of trade are far superior to approaches that increase the velocity of money. You will see that removing barriers to trade is what allows communities (and their citizens) to exchange things they have for things they want (or need). On the other hand, you will recognize most strategies that increase the velocity of money only serve to blow up volatility, ratchet up uncertainty, and expand the gaps in equality between the elites and the impoverished. However, it will anger you when you realize certain policies do nothing but favor one group of stakeholders in a supply chain at the expense of others. It will frustrate you when excessive regulations (fees, permits, paperwork, etc.) do more to benefit the rule makers versus the people who actually participate in the circle of trade. You will observe policies that seem to exist solely to allocate resources (natural resources, people and money) in the most inefficient way possible, perpetuating stagnation that guarantees healthy capital dies a slow death. You will witness good policies that are not enforced and bad policies that destroy human rights and other freedoms. You will appreciate policies that exist to enhance the safety of those in a community. Though you will realize that no policy can protect everyone from every risk that might endanger a human being. In time, you will acknowledge good policy is what cements the other forces (resources, infrastructure, price and education, or R~I~P~E) in a coherent strategy that provides a more harmonious life for each member of a community. Policy is the only force that can weave culture into a well-defined identity that represents all members of a community.

PRICE

Price is the metric that facilitates exchanges among people and their related communities. Typically, price is measured based on the legal currency that has been approved by a community. For example, in the United States, as well as throughout most of the world, the U.S. Dollar (the Dollar) is how one determines the price of something. For all practical purposes, at least today, the Dollar is the fundamental unit to measure the amount of money in the same way a second is the fundamental measurement of time. Moreover, when it comes to labor, a significant input into the final price of most products and services, price is measured with respect to a unit of time (wage rate per hour).

Since price is the metric we use for exchange, it is also the principle tool to measure relative value. For example, if you pay $150,000 for your home and $30,000 for your car, then the relative value of your home is 5 times greater than your car. If you earn $100 an hour for your time and another individual is paid $20 for an hour for their labor, then your relative value of your time is 5 times more valuable than the other individual. Most individuals never think in terms of relative values unless they are involved in a barter transaction (exchanging goods or services, for example, trading food for the labor to build one's shelter) or they believe the relative value of a person's time is not fair (what a CEO earns relative to the average worker).

Everyone values time and therefore all of us factor this variable into many of our decisions. Companies in a competitive market (their focus is on the consumer) also understand this preference. Consequently, they will embrace technology and improve processes so our buying experience and product/service enjoyment will be more pleasant (shorter lines, faster checkouts, clear instructions, ease of use, etc.). In a relative sense, such companies understand the importance of delivering greater value to the consumer in conjunction with lowering their cost of delivery. Companies that are not in a competitive market (their focus is on the producer) have less incentive to make the consumer experience enjoyable. Consequently, in a relative sense, not only are prices higher (unless heavily subsidized) but the time consumers spend with respect to the product/service (buying, using, receiving, maintaining, repairing, etc.) is much greater. **Most of us don't assign a value to the time we squander** (that is, time we could have spent with our family, friends or ourselves). **However, time lost represents a significant amount of waste to ourselves, to our loved ones and to our communities.**

Many economists think of price in terms of traditional diagrams of supply and demand curves for particular goods and services. Although important, I want you to begin to think of price more in terms of a community's supply chains with price representing the total value that accrues to all of the individuals that belong to a particular economic group.

A supply chain is the best way to picture a market and therefore includes everyone who participates in the production and delivery of a good or service. A simple supply chain would include a producer, a consumer and an agent (a retailer or salesperson) that might connect the two. A more complex supply chain would include other parties that would take a piece of the economic pie, such as creators or inventors (royalties or licensing fees), regulators (fees, permits and taxes) and providers of capital (interest and dividends). The relative percentage each party receives from (or pays into) a supply chain is a good barometer to measure the pricing power and influence of each stakeholder. Every person you can think of and every entity you can identify is a participant in hundreds of different supply chains, some with very little degrees of separation. All of these complimentary and competing supply chains represent the Circle of Commerce that drives the economies of all communities.

The primary economic objective of all communities (whether the community is one individual or a collection of many individuals) is to maximize value from the supply chain that impacts them the most. Most of the time, this is a zero sum game. If you win, someone else loses. Only in the most elementary exchange would a transaction make some better off while leaving no one worse off.

Many times it is very difficult, especially over a longer time horizon, to project who will actually receive the ultimate benefit of a price change and what parties will feel the pain of pricing decisions made today (today's "winners" might be tomorrow's "losers"). Moreover, there are thousands of variables (not only prices) that impact the interaction between and among homogenous and hetero-geneous communities. It is impossible to determine what price changes would overall, if any, benefit the broadest community (a world economy of 7 billion plus individuals). In the longer term, a change in relative values will reflect the complex interaction leaders have on policies that im-pact a community's overall stability. Depending on which communities win, and which communities lose, the world economy might be relatively better off, or worse off.

If we benefit from a price change (higher wages or lower costs of consumption) we are usually oblivious, or we don't care, what happens to others in the supply chain (e.g. the inexpensive clothes I buy which are made under horren-dous labor conditions in Bangladesh). On the other hand, price changes that are detrimental to us might cause us to identify those who we believe benefit at our expense (rising gas prices caused by greedy oil companies). In other words, most of us focus on our own interests, which may be selfish or altruistic. Even if one stakeholder is able to improve the outcome of other stakeholders, some stakeholders in the supply chain will always believe they are worse off.

The entities that maximize the amount of money from the supply chain are those with the most power to influ-ence outcomes. Consequently, in a complex supply chain prices can never be "fair" because the stakeholders in the supply chain all have a different view of fairness. Or, to say it a different way; **the individuals or communities in power determine what is fair.** The communities in power are those that control resources, infrastructure and policy which include those individuals that have relevant skills or connections. It's not surprising, when entities are threatened by competitive forces that might lower price, they hire as many lobbyists as necessary to enact federal legislation or state regulation that helps to protect them.

When an entity's total price of its outputs exceed the total price of its inputs an entity will generate a profit. Profits are critical to every entity because it provides the money to invest in the entity's future, or the future of others. Moreover, to the extent an investment was funded with debt, then profits are the only means to repay the debt and the related interest costs on that debt. Consequently, unless we intend to rely on the charity of others, all of us are capitalists because every entity needs to generate savings today to increase the likelihood of stability tomorrow. Savings (wealth) as you learned earlier, is the property you own and the skills you acquire. Hypocrisy reins when leaders believe losses (the opposite of profits) are a better way to secure future happiness. Deficits always need to be financed by someone, sowing the seeds of an entity's future dependency.

Therefore, the question is not whether an organization should generate a profit (savings for the future). The question is how should this profit be shared among all stakeholders. At the extremes, government controlled entities sacrifice (or trade-off) profits at the expense of efficiencies; private entities optimize profits by maximizing efficiencies. The conundrum arises when certain stakeholders believe profits are not shared on an equitable basis (workers are underpaid; executives are overpaid) and efficiencies are being minimized (usually at the expense of the customer) or maximized (usually for the benefit of the investors).

Communities then use various policies to shift prices in an effort to resolve this conundrum.

When products and/or services are given away for free, either; (a) someone else in the supply chain has borne the cost of the freeness (b) the "free" stuff was essentially bundled with other things that the consumer actually bought, (c) the consumer exchanged something that has little or no value to them (e.g. their time, privacy, etc.), or (d) they have incurred some form of obligation that will manifest itself in the future (e.g. "free" financing). The wealthier a community, the greater its ability to deliver (and to sustain such delivery in the future) products or services as public goods that are either free or heavily subsidized (healthcare; education, energy, food, etc.).

Truth is, most of the time, somebody is subsidizing someone else in a supply chain. For example, seniors might subsidize the young (the price of education), the youth might subsidize the seniors (the price of healthcare), the responsible might subsidize the reckless (insurance), savers might subsidize debtors (the return on assets versus the price of debt), and workers might subsidize the pay of executives. Most people only focus on a subsidy when they are not the beneficiary.

Prices today seldom reflect externalities, especially when it relates to environmental costs and other expenses that will be incurred in the future by those who benefit from the product or service. The price of cigarettes does not include a fee used to fund the future healthcare cost of smokers. The price of nuclear power does not include the cost to shut down reactors that become obsolete or no longer can be maintained. In the rare occasion where taxes are collected for such purposes the money received is usually spent for other endeavors. Societies have a long history of privatizing profits and nationalizing losses. You should not expect this to change in the future.

Every stakeholder will use a variety of tools to move prices in their favor in order to improve the outcomes for their constituents. The entity with the greatest tools to influence price is government. Therefore stakeholders, using their connections with politicians, will lobby (often referred to as rent seeking) for those tools that will provide their constituents the greatest benefit. These tools include the ability to regulate, control, manipulate and set prices for capital (e.g. currency and interest rates), labor (e.g. wages, hours and licensing requirements), products/services (e.g. taxes, fees, penalties, subsidies, duties, tariffs, price controls, and price support) as well as government's active participation in an economy's most significant markets (finance, insurance, housing, education, healthcare, and energy).

National governments also have the unique power to create money to facilitate the exchange of goods and services and to increase the funds available for it to spend. The price of this money is a reflection of a number of variables. Low interest rates on U.S. government bonds, for example, could reflect a confidence in the long-term policy decisions of a nation's leaders, an unorthodox monetary policy (the only buyer of the nation's debt is the government) and/or a flight to safety by investors who believe their own currencies are at risk.

When the populist is unhappy, a national government is especially active in managing the money supply and prices. For example, if an individual's wages are decreasing (deflation) during a time when their cost of living is increasing (inflation), then the decline in a community's overall standard of living will prompt a national government to distort prices in the hope it can alleviate such concerns. This distortion could be in various forms, but usually involves subsidies that lower the cost of goods that consumers demand (independent of changes in supply) or wage increases that benefit the producer and are passed on to the consumer in the form of price increases (independent of changes in demand).

In contrast, where there is minimal government involvement (in early 2015 the unregulated Internet was one of the few markets left with limited government intervention), stakeholders in a supply chain will rely on other tools to influence prices. Producers can use monopolies and cartels; consumers can resort to boycotts and other forms of protest; and workers can form unions or participate in various forms of activism. Moreover, financial players (principally hedge funds), which are totally outside a traditional supply chain, can hoard, store, speculate and participate in other forms of price manipulation driven by changes in the global money supply. And, of course, let's not forget those tools most of us would deem illegal, such as bribes, kickbacks and other forms of coercion.

In most supply chains, all of these tools might drive a change in supply and demand, or a change in supply or demand might drive a need for such tools. Given the complexity of today's markets, and the ongoing battle among stakeholders to improve outcomes for their constituents, only the simplest of markets establish prices based on a pure laissez-faire free market interaction among participants.

Therefore, in any pricing model there are numerous inputs that impact price and there are numerous inputs that impact supply and impact demand, including R-I-P-P-L-E-S cost models that vary dramatically among communities. All of these inputs, in some manner, impact a market and therefore "distort" a market price. Even instant and ubiquitous price discovery that transfers the power of information from the producer to the consumer will not elimination this distortion. In other words, there is no process that allocates resources in a manner that is fair to all communities.

As a result, **the price of any product or service is nothing more than "the price."** Individuals will always disagree on what is the "true" price, the ""fair" price, the "equilibrium" price, the "market" price or the "real" price depending on what price an individual believes is the best price that maximizes value for members of a particular community. Value based pricing is especially tricky because everyone measures value differently. The "right" price for a consumer could slide up or down from a producer's "optimal" price based on different preferences chosen by each consumer. Moreover, price is often only one variable in a supply chain that actually determines who receives a good or buys a service. I might agree to pay the price for a MBA from the University of Chicago ("UC") but UC could still choose not to accept me into their program.

Prices influence how people behave and how people behave influences prices. This behavior drives the allocation of resources, the investment in infrastructure, the composition of policies and best practices in education. If leaders mix these ingredients wisely, a community has a greater likelihood of achieving stability and maintaining this equilibrium during periods of volatility. If not, then communities will experience smuggling, undocumented workers, private bartering, and other signs of a shadowy black market. At the right price people learn how to get what they want, independent of the channel that might actually deliver the product or service.

Rational communities want stable prices that reflect a rising standard of living and increasing quality of life for its members. Inflation that significantly increases wages (without increases in output or productivity) will make every product and service in the community's supply chain cost more. On the other hand, significant deflation typically results in hoarding cash and delaying investments. Both extremes send unfavorable ripples throughout a community with adverse outcomes for most of its members.

Increase the price of a scarce resource and people will use less of it. Legalize and tax illicit activities and people will come out of the shadows. Subsidize energy costs and people will waste more fuel and electricity. Cap apartment rents and investors will build fewer properties. The difficulty is how to predict behavior when members of a community have many different priorities and preferences.

As you move through the next decade you will recognize the most important price is your own personal exchange rate. You will learn your personal spending patterns will be much different from published inflation rates and yet the rate that relative prices increase will still pose the greatest risk to your community's independence. **Every decision you make in the natural course of events will have an economic impact of some magnitude.** Whether you get married, go to college, start a family, buy a car, or rent a home, each of these decisions impact the price of that particular product or service and ripples through various communities. All products and services will eventually clear a market at some price, but seldom will that price appear fair to all participants. It will surprise you that almost all prices have been distorted for someone's benefit, but a lack of transparency will often make it difficult to identify who exactly received the benefit. It will disappoint you when government uses prices to reward rent seekers instead of promoting more efficient global commerce. However, you will realize price has its greatest force in shaping a community only when consumers have the freedom to make their own choices and bear the benefits, risks and consequences of those decisions.

LEADERS

Upon reflection, all of you will acknowledge that you have led some group of individuals and certainly you have followed the leadership of others. What I want you to understand is what really matters is how you lead and how others lead you. How you lead changes depending on who you lead. Who you follow depends on how they lead you. Soon you will appreciate why there are very few great leaders. Within the communities you value, I hope you become one of those leaders.

What is a Leader? A Leader is a person that members of a community look to for advice, counsel and direction and sadly this would include any individual that has almost God-like control over their constituents.

An effective leader has a vision for tomorrow and knows how to influence members of a community to behave in such a manner that allows the community to pursue and achieve this vision. If successful, this persuasion melts into a culture of shared values forming the bridge that

> **Everyone leads someone. It's how you lead and why you lead that matters.**

ultimately connects all members of the community. Therefore, successful leaders are always asking themselves:

- What outcomes do they want?
- What is the best way to persuade an individual (or a group of individuals) to behave in a way that increases the likelihood that those goals are met?

The scariest leaders are those who have no idea what type of outcomes they want as they fumble their way through bizarre helter-skelter decision making that leaves their constituents totally bewildered. These schizoid leaders compete with other crazed rulers who might actually know what outcomes they want, but totally underestimate the trade-offs and consequences of achieving their vision.

With respect to the effectiveness of a leader it doesn't matter whether the outcome is good or bad. For example, one could argue both Hitler and Churchill used various behavior techniques to achieve certain desired outcomes. In other words, an effective leader could be virtuous or evil. Leaders who achieve positive outcomes for their community might be labeled good, even if such an outcome was detrimental to some of its constituents or harmful to members of other communities. Communities that have negative outcomes might label their leaders bad, even if the leader generally possesses positive moral characteristics.

Since luck, chance and uncertainty all have an impact on outcomes, today's successful leaders might be tomorrow's losers and today's "losers" might be the successful leaders in the future. In addition, a leader who achieves positive outcomes in one environment might experience negative outcomes in other arenas (the leader could be a lousy parent). Moreover, an effective leader could have underlying personal character flaws (he or she could be a disloyal spouse, a crack smoking addict, a functional alcoholic, etc.) that may or may not undermine their longer-term leadership potential. In other words, a "successful" leader in one domain might be an "awful" leader in a different environment.

It is this understanding of human behavior that impacts how a leader predicts, changes or responds to the people he or she leads and to others who are outside of the community. For example, some people respond to tough love performance reviews that lay bare an individual's flaws. Others, however, respond better to positive feedback that reinforces their strengths while encouraging more attention to shoring up their weaknesses.

A Leader's ability to influence the behavior of a person, or more importantly the behavior of a group, is why many leaders share common personality traits that include excellent communication skills, an engaging persona and an enchanting charisma (they are performers in a world desperately seeking video sound-bites). However, leaders who demonstrate professionalism, competence, integrity and persuade with quiet humility, or those who sadly motivate through a culture of fear, may have none of these attributes. All leaders compete with other leaders (no matter how small their communities) for power and influence.

Leadership is difficult because human behavior is complex and often very hard to predict. Leaders scan our brains, analyze our clicks, record our movements, track our spending, map our relationships, survey our opinions, monitor our health, investigate our transgressions, and document our performance. The results of these activities, along with many others, are sliced into numerous demographic and social economical groups. Despite the Orwellian creepiness of it all, it is this research that provides the insight into why different groups of people behave the way they do. Behavioral research, of course, does not have to be based on facts. For example, if people believe vaccines cause autism, genetically modified seeds are bad for you and humans cause global warming, then certain leaders can use this knowledge to further specific agendas. In other words, behavior is driven by beliefs. Whether such beliefs are supported by facts or truths does not impact the behavior.

During my senior year in high school, all college-bound students, were required to compete in the local Science Fair. As my peers designed elaborate projects in biology, chemistry, and other traditional sciences, my skeptical advisor, after much discussion among the faculty, approved my project in Subliminal Stimuli. I don't think anyone expected much from my endeavor, but with the help of my mother and the advertising firm where she worked, I was able to design a number of experiments that showed how sex and violence were being used to manipulate our behavior using our subconscious minds. I was the only one in our class to the travel to the State Science Fair in Columbus, Ohio and received a perfect score for my efforts (much to the horror, I suspect, of my science teacher). It appeared all of the judges were fascinated by how an innocuous ice cube in a picture of an alcoholic drink was arousing our sexual fantasies. Bacardi Rum never tasted so good!

Leaders understand these nuances. They recognize information (including the manipulation of it) is valuable and those who can control and shape statistics and other data (whether rumors, propaganda, fact or fiction) are the ones who ultimately filter the knowledge that impacts public opinion. Leaders also understand deep-seated ideologies and beliefs are very difficult to change once they have been ingrained within a particular community. Using this knowledge of human nature, combined with the power to allocate resources, build infrastructure, make policy, determine price, control education and influence stability, is how leaders persuade, sway, motivate and otherwise convince us to behave in a manner that achieves a desired outcome. Some may argue none of us can act against our own desires (we have no free will) but leaders understand the easiest way for a four year old to resist a tasty chocolate chip cookie is not to offer one.

Independent of outcomes, all of us have our own views as to what makes a "bad" leader. For example, as we discussed earlier, when leaders limit your freedoms and begin to control what you hear, what you read, what you watch, how you think, how you feel, what you earn and how you spend, then a community takes on more cult-like characteristics. In essence, community members become brainwashed by their iconic sociopathic leaders, the sellers of dreams, and as the populist descends into darkness, the leaders purge the nonbelievers as part of the process. Bad leaders are like the Varroa mite, a bloodsucking parasite.

Many of us would also consider leaders who lie, cheat, coerce, deceive, seduce and utilize other forms of manipulation or fear, to influence our behavior, as corrupt. No one likes to be tricked into behaving in a certain matter. Corrupt leaders always lose sight of those they actually represent as they pursue their own selfish concerns and special interests. Seldom do they measure, or even consider, the consequences of their conflicted decisions and how it might impact those who believed and trusted in their leadership. Fortunately, once they lose their sterling reputations they seldom recover. Sadly, the most dangerous leaders are those who actually believe what they are doing is good, and yet leave nothing but human suffering and tragedy in their wake.

All leaders have power and therefore, by their very nature, at least in a specific domain, they are Elite. Leaders team with other Elites (those who control Resources or Infrastructure) for purposes of making the most important decisions (influencing Policy, Price and Education) for any community. The greater the population of a community (and/or the more interaction with neighboring communities), the more difficult it is for the Elites to make decisions that balance the wishes of all of its members. Larger communities have multiple stakeholders (all of which have their leaders) who have revolving roles that reflect different (and often competing or complementary) interests. These roles can include, but are not limited to: employer-employee, owner-worker, soldier-officer, producer-consumer, seller-buyer, parent-child, teacher-student, doctor-patient, politician-taxpayer, bureaucrat-voter, debtor-creditor, criminal-law enforcement, lawyer-client, judge-juror, etc. Most decisions appear to favor one group of stakeholders versus another because all of us have different perspectives and/or priorities.

Most leaders that you follow were selected with no input from you and yet you are accountable to them. For example, your parents, your teachers, your coaches, your professors and your boss were not persons you choose to lead you. It's a reminder that great leaders do not have to be elected by those they lead. Absolute monarchs, like all leaders, can be benevolent or savage and often dictatorships are the best way (and sometimes the only way) to optimize the effectiveness and efficiency of a community.

The only system that allows you to have input into and actually allows you, and the other members of your community, to select the individual that will lead you, is a democracy. Usually there is some form of competition among people who want to lead, but a democracy is the system in which all of the people of a community have the opportunity to elect their leader. However, democratic elections for large communities seldom elect great leaders because of a lack of qualified candidates or overall voter apathy (low voter turnout). That is, community members recognize many candidates cannot be trusted because they will say, do or become whatever is necessary to sway voters to elect them. Nevertheless, a democracy requires the leader to be accountable to the electorate and consequently, if they are not, the citizens can eventually remove them from power. The leaders of a representative democracy (like the United States) have the most difficult assignment (of any leader) because often times, they have dualistic responsibilities that conflict.

Do they represent the communities who voted for them, or the interests of all the people (the common good)? Do they stand by their principles, or support the special interests of those who financed their campaigns? Do they represent the taxpayers or those who depend on the taxpayers? Do they represent the voice of the producers or the wishes of the consumers? Do they help the employers or protect the employees? Do they educate the youth or take care of the old? Do they support the majority or defend the minority? Every member of the community is also a member of one, or more than one, of these competing and complementary groups of people. It is because of these conflicts and competing interests and agendas that elected politicians, more so than other leaders, have an extremely difficult time appeasing members of their community.

If you are going to elect effective Leaders, or if you choose to follow the wisdom of others, you must understand a Leader's fundamental beliefs and map those with your most important values and your vision of tomorrow. That is, you need to understand what they believe so you will have better insight into how they will behave and therefore how they will lead.

For example, if I were to lead a community, there are certain core principles I would consider with respect to every community decision. I would protect the community's most precious and scarce natural resources. I would build and maintain infrastructure that would enhance trade among members of my community and our neighbors. I would require transparency of all public monies spent on behalf of private citizens. I would let competition among producers and choice among consumers set prices for most goods and services. I would cap the community's money supply. I would develop innovative learning programs for today based on the types of jobs we want for tomorrow. I would have all elected leaders of the community sign a professional code of conduct. I would educate, not regulate. I would simplify, not mystify. I would arbitrate, not litigate. I would emphasize equal opportunity, not equality.

I would only make commitments that have a reasonable likelihood of coming true. I would let the members of the community enjoy the benefits and suffer the consequences of the choices they make. These are some examples of my views with respect to how I might (because trade-offs are often complex) lead a community.

When you study community successes and failures you will quickly agree the most important skill of an elected leader is to shape the policies that are the most mission critical to the prosperity and sustainability of their communities. You will witness leaders who nurture an entrepreneurial spirit among their constituents and therefore provide their communities the most vibrant of economies. Such leaders recognize it is the entrepreneurs (along with inventors and other change makers) who create the jobs that drive trade and consumer choice. As such, these leaders foster an environment where risks that produce success are rewarded and the community respects the personal and intellectual property rights of its citizens and their businesses.

Conflicts will always be easier to resolve within a community that shares common values and ideologies. Conflicts are much more difficult to successfully resolve when they involve different communities with competing views and interests. Great leaders (which are extremely rare) have a unique ability to resolve such conflicts because they listen and consider the views of others. Such leaders will change their views in a belief that alternative outcomes may be more fair and equitable to all individuals; not just the normal selfish interests of the constituents they represent. In other words, they redefine winning in a much broader context.

You will smile when you identify leaders who embrace transparency, a fresh look, diverse views, debate and compromise. These leaders endorse a free and open media because they know it is the best way to ensure human rights and to keep them honest in the process. They understand the importance of understanding the interests of all constituents. You will be angry when you observe people trampled by cruel and repressive leaders. It will bother you to observe leaders who successfully lie, deceive, obfuscate, manipulate, coerce and basically use any and every means available to stay in power. It will disturb you that rational thought will not sway individuals who think and behave irrationally. But you will rejoice when the masses seize control and nominate (or elect) those leaders who can mint character in others and communicate an ideology that is shared by the masses. Then, and only then, will you understand it is those leaders who reward meritocracy whom are able to build communities that have success in closing the gaps of inequality.

EDUCATION

I want you to take a couple of minutes, clear your thoughts of any traditional views of education, and totally rethink how one defines education. Then ask yourself this very important question — Why do we educate? Why is education for you so important to your mother and me? We must agree on the why, so we can begin to agree on the what (What do we teach?) and the how (How do we teach?). If I bumped into a relative I had not seen for years and she asked, "How are the boys? Are they educated?" How would I answer? I would answer, "It depends."

Why should **we educate** you? In my view, there is only one primary reason: **so you can make better choices and decisions during your life.** If you can't apply tomorrow what you learn today, then, what is the value? Once you understand education is a process of life long learning it is easier to recognize that it is not possible to be truly educated since every day brings a brand new learning experience. Therefore, the important question is not whether someone has an education, it is whether the person has been equipped with the tools necessary to pursue a process of lifetime learning. In other words, **are you learning how to learn?**

What are these tools? The depth and breadth of your toolbox is a function of what choices you will trust others to make on your behalf and what decisions you intend to make yourself. Essentially, you will seesaw between a continuum that traverses a path of dependence and independence. Of course, the people you trust can make bad choices for you. Similarly, you can certainly make bad decisions for yourself. As you balance on this teeter totter called life you will begin to recognize your most important decisions, whether good or bad,

A thirst for wisdom is the only thing that protects you from the cults who poison the drinks of their followers.

weave health, career, relationships, and finance into a rich tapestry of daily choices that shape your future.

An individual's education and learning process is a reflection of the community that raises him. If a community has minimal natural resources, poor infrastructure, policies that restrict trade, prices that benefit producers and/ or leaders that are corrupt, then a person's toolbox is usually limited to the minimal skills necessary to perpetuate a morbid existence. On the other hand, if a community has vast natural resources, excellent infrastructure, policies that promote the exchange of ideas, prices that benefit consumers, and leaders that are noble, then the person is usually aptly rewarded for developing a robust toolbox of skills that will facilitate a lifetime of learning.

Communities that don't educate must be more paternalistic because their members will be constantly making wrong choices, including bad economic decisions. Often the uneducated appear irrational and foolish. Truth is, many of them lack the basic information necessary to make the best decision. However, even with the right information many people will not make decisions that are in their best interests, or in the best interests of their community. This is why leaders, for example, implement new policies to remove fatty choices from one's diet, instead of educating obese citizens on the merits of eating healthier foods. **If you can't educate, then you must regulate.**

Parents, usually with the assistance of other family members, represent the primary community that has the awesome responsibility to nurture and guide our youth in an environment that enriches them with opportunities to learn and explore.

To learn you need to be healthy; therefore nutritious meals, daily exercise, childhood immunizations, and a safe environment formed the cornerstones of your early upbringing. To communicate, you need to read, write and speak. So we read to you early and often, teaching you how to articulate and recognize the English language which eventually led to your intense desire to read and write on your own. To understand money you need to use math. So we used coins to teach you how to add and subtract, dice to teach how to multiply and divide and card games like Poker to teach you how to calculate outcomes and refine your memory skills. To problem solve, you needed to distinguish patterns from noise and therefore we taught you how to play games like Chess, Monopoly, Risk and Clue. To think rationally you needed to understand the scientific

method, so everyday was a continuous dialogue of cause
and effect. To develop relationships, you needed to interact
with others, so we pushed you into youth sports and other
communities that facilitated peer interface. To understand
human behavior, we taught you a sense of right and wrong
and how to lead a moral life. Communication, the value
of money, problem solving, rational thought, relationship
building and personal integrity were some of the first skills
that went into your early toolbox of lifetime learning.

**One of the primary reasons you learn how to
learn is so you can develop skills you can trade for
things you want or need.** However, whether the skills
you develop match your real talent is a function of two
variables. First, how well the leaders of a community have
developed (or intend to develop) the resources, infrastructure, and policies that allow you to pursue your passion
and unique talents. Second, whether there is a price arbitrage. In other words, is it reasonably possible the value
of your future earnings will exceed the actual cost of your
investment, including the opportunity cost of your time?

In most communities, there is no process or system to
manage the current or future needs of the economy with
the skills required of its workers. In an economy as deep
and broad as the U.S. this can create either a tremendous
benefit or terrible detriment to its citizens. For those few
individuals who have a core team of talented career advisors (e.g. parents, mentors, teachers, friends, etc.) coupled
with the freedom of movement, there is a reasonable
chance their talents will be channeled in a direction where
they have the greatest opportunity to benefit themselves
and their community.

On the other hand, for those desperate souls which are
left to fend for themselves, there is a pretty good chance
they will not develop the skills that maximize their real
talents and best career opportunities. This is especially

true if they lack the freedom, or the desire, to move out of a smaller community that has few, or declining, opportunities. Some will accept legitimate low paying jobs for menial labor. Others will rely on the generosity of their communities. Many will develop the skills that will allow them to survive in the shadow economy that perpetuates a life of crime in the dark markets of the underworld (in other words, such individuals will take advantage of the only opportunities that are available to them).

In most communities, unskilled workers are significantly greater in number than those workers with the skills that a community values. Such a situation will always increase inequality, especially in a merit-based society. This increase in inequality occurs for two major reasons.

First, as demand chases the supply of skilled workers, wages tend to spiral upwards. Conversely, when there is an excess supply of unskilled workers, wages for those individuals tend to stay flat or decline (assuming that the unskilled worker still has a job). Skilled workers, who have the greatest opportunity to generate savings have the added benefit of earning a return on their capital as well as their labor.

Second, basic necessities make up a larger and larger percentage of the total costs of living for the unskilled workers versus the skilled workers. It's not possible for unskilled workers to have the same relative level of savings because basic necessities of life make up a higher percentage of their daily living costs. In fact, unskilled workers will borrow, if they can; not necessarily because they want to but often because they have to. That is, borrowing is the only way to secure the funds necessary to sustain any reasonable standard of living.

When the average wage rate for a skilled worker begins to reach parity with the unskilled worker, then the value of those with skills will be equal to those individuals who lack skills. When this parity persists, for whatever reason (corrupt leaders, bad policies, poor education and an unstable environment), there will be minimal incentives for those with unique talents to develop those skills (if for no other reason then they will lack sufficient resources and infrastructure). Declines in performance and productivity will follow and eventually a community that previously embraced meritocracy will slip into a stagnant shadow of doom. In other words, when policy is all about jobs, and not productivity, then all a community gets is a lot of unproductive jobs.

It's sad in so many ways. I sometimes wonder how much better off our society might be if we had as many career advisors as financial advisors. In other words, a greater emphasis on increasing the value of the worker and a bit less on maximizing the return on the money supply. In a merit based world, the best way to close the equality gap is to increase the skills of the workforce. Perhaps not surprising, as parents it was always important to us, and it still is, that others are chasing you and not the other way around. Achievement gaps, especially from early childhood, are very difficult to close in high school and almost impossible at the university level. These gaps only become wider when the youth of a community are making poor career choices.

The good news is that those who learn how to learn are the trailblazers who invent the jobs of tomorrow that expand the depth and breadth of products and services that a community can trade. Dynamic communities embrace, support and facilitate these inventors because they recognize if they don't, then other communities will. It is through education that communities develop such benefits as clean energy and state-of-the-art healthcare services.

Innovation will happen, either in your community or somewhere else. So communities have a choice; (1) develop the technology and the related products/services and export this knowledge to others, or (2) import these items, once they become available, from competing communities. Technology drives innovation but, more importantly, it accelerates our ability to learn. Even today, throughout the world, kids who are 3 years old (i.e. recently born in 2012!) operate iPhone apps, know a web address, open a browser, play online games and answer a cell phone.

As you mature you will see the most successful communities are those where the people are free to pursue a life of perpetual learning. It is those people who are in the best position to contribute to a representative government. You will understand the task of becoming educated is never ending. You will begin to believe perennial learning is the path to innovation and innovation is what creates tomorrow's opportunities. You will discover societies which embrace technology are the ones that increase the productivity of all resources (e.g. natural resources that deliver more value; labor that generates greater output; and money that is allocated to the most worthwhile and efficient endeavors) so all of us can enjoy more, by consuming less. You will realize that if your community develops better products and services, then this is something they can export and trade with others. And, if you do not, then you will be forced to import the technology and related products and services; fertilizing the seeds of your dependency.

It will irritate you when those in power perpetuate a culture of ignorance to make it easier for them to exploit the naïve and uneducated. It will anger you to witness societies who teach students from curriculum that have no relevance to the jobs of tomorrow. It will frustrate you that many students must go to college to obtain even the most basic skills that employers crave. It will sadden you to observe communities who hire people based on who they know (i.e. relationships) and not what they know (i.e.

competence). It will bother you when people with talent are abandoned and left to fend for themselves in the dungeons of the dark economy. However, in the end, you will discover that education that fuels the human spirit will ultimately nurture a caring community towards happiness.

STABILITY

Before we dig deeper into this concept called Stability, I want to digress for a moment and discuss a business venture that I started after leaving FirstCom in the latter half of 2000. The company was called *Praedictio.*

Praedictio was a business concept that was founded on the idea that companies could better use data analytics to assess the probability that a given future event would occur at a particular point at a particular time. Using a business framework of Discover – Model – Evaluate, *Praedictio's* mission was to provide proprietary services that would allow businesses to more accurately predict significant future events. These services would include tools, processes, workshops, and methodologies that impacted the entire prediction process. It was my belief that the usefulness of validating the past (for example, an audit of historical financial statements) would give way to a more dynamic need to better predict tomorrow's outcomes. If *Praedictio* could help companies more clearly see the future with better data, then it would be easier for a company to optimize profits in a more volatile environment. *Praedictio* would employ a team of futurists. A professional services firm hierarchical structure of staff, senior, manager and Partner would give way to a new matrix of people with titles such as Explorers, Scanners, Sensors, Surveyors, Interpreters, Synthesizers, Chartists, Designers, Examiners, Monitors and Inspectors.

For various reasons, *Praedictio* never evolved beyond it's original business plan. However, as we know, in 2015 almost everyone is in the prediction business. With the explosion of data analytics, all of us are trying to make better decisions about tomorrow's risks. Today's model builders understand humans are irrational. All of us have our biases that create strange interactions between randomness and causality. This is why outcomes are so difficult to predict. With respect to R~I~P~P~L~E, Stability is the outcome one hopes to achieve when the multiple variables that impact Resources, Infrastructure, Policy, Price, Leaders and Education are woven into the complex algorithms that impact all communities.

To understand this complexity, think about March Madness, the NCAA College Basketball Tournament. Sixty-eight teams compete over a period of weeks in the hope of being crowned The National Champion. To achieve the perfect bracket, one needs to predict the correct outcome of 67 games; in other words, you need to be right only 67 times. In 2015, more than 11.5 million people entered ESPN's Tournament Challenge. Guess how many people had a perfect bracket after the first round of 36 games. Well, one quarter of 1%. And, after the second round no one had a perfect bracket. So, what do you think is harder to achieve? A perfect bracket in the NCAA Basketball Tournament or Stability among all of the world's communities?

Stability, for any community, is a consequence of a constant, almost kaleidoscopic interplay, of resources, infrastructure, policies, price, leaders and education among all communities. Every community has a unique stability model because no two communities have exactly the same inputs (or the same outside forces that influence these inputs). Moreover, because imperfect people design, build, execute and interpret the models, it is not possible to have a perfect outcome when the process almost guarantees mistakes, misunderstandings and mismanagement.

As the size and number of communities increase, global stability is difficult to sustain because **the stability of many communities requires the instability of other communities.** This uncertainty is magnified when people who are unstable (who may be referred to as troublemakers) become part of the equation that impacts a community's stability. Leaders, as we discussed earlier, will use various behavior modification techniques (including medication) in the hope such individuals will wander through life in a zombie like mental state while conforming within a communities social norms and values. When the citizens don't conform, the community moves closer to chaos.

A stable community reflects a tranquil environment where members of a community can live happy and peaceful lives that are in harmony with those around them. However, enlightened communities that achieve stability recognize their current state of bliss represents a fragile equilibrium between stagnation and chaos. Their leaders understand they teeter on a delicate precipice between tyranny and liberty, misery and prosperity, and peace and war.

Utopia cannot exist in a world where many people hate their neighbors because of ideological, economic or social differences. It's why genocidal evil decimated the Jews in Europe, massacred the middle class in the killing fields of Cambodia, and slaughtered children in Rwanda. Mass violence has almost become a way of life for those miserable and unfortunate souls forced to fight for survival in Burma, Sudan, Libya and throughout the Middle East.

This inability to maintain stability is what I call the Paradox of Peace. The Paradox of Peace recognizes that human behavior is volatile and therefore the probability of achieving a stable environment for all mankind is equivalent to the probability of a world in perpetual chaos. Both have the same likelihood at any given moment. An environment where the flip of a coin is often the ultimate arbitrator of one's fate. An environment that accepts, for example, that radical violent extremists and nonviolent advocates for basic human rights will never co-exist harmoniously.

I wish it was different and there was a more compelling way for the entire human race to live and work together in some broader symbiotic relationship. Unfortunately, the fundamental characteristics that seem to survive thousands of years of human evolution are the "seven deadly sins" of pride, envy, gluttony, lust, anger, greed, and sloth. One can debate whether such behaviors are "deadly" or "sinful" but there is no question that such behaviors, and a host of others (including pure evil that seems to manifest itself in a greater percentage of the population), will ensure perpetual instability for many communities and their members.

To achieve (and hopefully sustain) stability, every community needs a strong anchor. This anchor can manifest itself as a key resource, strong infrastructure, sound polices, fair prices, great leaders or terrific education. Strong anchors help communities build resiliency and leverage during periods of uncertainty. The more anchors, the more stable the community. However, as the currents of tomorrow change, as the ripples grow stronger or weaker, the anchors need to adapt, evolve and change. If not, then the community's economic and social foundations crumble, leaving chaos in its wake.

Of course, the control of one force will never guarantee stability of any community. For example, communities with valuable natural resources cannot leverage such resources without proper infrastructure. Proper infrastructure requires leaders to establish policies that fairly allocate prices among all stakeholders in the supply chain. However, prices will never be fair if community members lack the education to make the most basic economic decisions. All of these forces need to work in a symbiotic relationship to provide any hope of stability. However, that said, there is no question certain communities today have a significant stability advantage over other communities. For example, the synergy and peacefulness of the states that comprise the United States, China and India is vastly different compared to the perpetual wars waged by many dysfunctional communities in Africa and the Middle East.

The opportunity for community stability will always be greater for those societies which have (a) an abundance of natural resources relative to their population and (b) the depth and breadth of people and/or money that enables them to protect their most precious resources. This protection can be in a variety of forms. For example, it could be rules that conserve natural resources, military supremacy that safeguards a certain way of life or policies that promote the soundness of a country's currency.

Members of communities (or members within a community) who lack resources (natural, people or money) to achieve a reasonable quality of life will always feel a certain amount of anger toward other communities that have higher standards of living. The more dependent they become on the charity of others, the more disenfranchised they will be. The younger members of the community, who see no hope for a better way of life, are usually the first to pick up the weapons of destruction. They may be naïve about many things, but they do understand that the benefit of vast resources of any community accrue to those who control it.

Today, the United States may be the only country in the world that has an abundance of all resources. All other communities, if they desire a comparable or even greater standard of living, must trade with others to achieve such outcomes (e.g., Norway, Saudi Arabia, Qatar, Israel, etc.). It's only through trade that smaller communities create the depth and breadth of alliances that will help them sustain some form of peaceful existence and reasonable standard of living for its members. Trade between large communities creates both comparative and competitive advantages that accrue to both entities over the short term. However, whether such trade flows actually benefit each economy (or the overall world economy) over the long term is difficult to assess since environmental degradation (or other long term threats to human health) is seldom factored in the cost of production or the price of consumerism. Moreover, in a complex supply chain it's impossible for trade to be efficient, because there will always be some stakeholders in each community who will be worse off.

Trade among smaller communities may also create some advantages. However, smaller communities which trade with similar communities create a certain amount of co-dependency among themselves. Small communities that trade with large communities give up a tremendous amount of independence in the hope their dependent relationship will make their members better off than they would have been without the exchange. Consequently, most small communities are inherently unstable because their stability is dependent on a stable relationships with others. Moreover, as communities become more unstable, the critical people that anchor a community (those with talent and those with money), if they are mobile, will eventually leave the community in search of a more stable environment (which accelerates a community's rate of instability until only chaos remains). Sadly, most communities that lack a depth and breadth of resources will never achieve lasting stability because they end up in a constant process of exchanging one form of dependency for another.

As you can see, most communities must trade with outsiders if they want to improve the standard of living for their members. The relative value of what a community can trade versus what it needs often results in a certain interdependence between trading partners and in some cases lead to a dependency relationship. In addition, one could also argue those who have an abundance of resources have an obligation to trade with other societies (even if it lowers the standard of living for the "richer" community) because this reallocation of resources creates more stable neighbors and therefore a more peaceful world. However, if a community is truly impoverished then "donations" should not be masked as trade. Instead, those with abundance should work with those less fortunate to develop better infrastructure, equitable policies, fair prices, virtuous leaders and practical education that allows these communities to produce something of value.

The overall efficiency (as a result of policy, price and education) of a community's resources (natural, people and money) and infrastructure will manifest themselves in the dependency ratio for a community. A community's dependency ratio is one of the most important metrics that determines whether a community can sustain a stable and peaceful environment.

Dependency ratios can vary among communities for a variety of reasons. However, in all cases lower dependency ratios that result in the highest standards of living are a result of policies enacted by leaders that optimize the complex relationships between resources, infrastructure, prices and the education of its citizens.

The dependency ratio is the relationship between those who produce (that is, workers) and those who do not (for example, the youth, elderly, unskilled, disabled and those who can't find a job). For example, in a three-generation family of 6 people, if the non workers include the father, 2 grandparents and 2 children (the mother is the only skilled worker), then the dependency ratio is 5 to 1. If two communities have identical natural resources, but one community has a higher dependency ratio, then the standard of living can only be equalized if the skilled worker in the community with the higher dependency ratio is more productive.

Unless a community has a tremendous amount of savings (sufficient to fund those who don't work), the workers must produce enough to sustain those who do not work. Moreover, communities with higher dependency ratios relative to other communities must generate greater worker productivity from those who do work, if they have any desire to close the gaps in the standards of living between communities. If the standard of living cannot be improved through greater worker productivity (there is no demand for what is produced, the workers have lost the desire to subsidize the non-workers or there is a culture of laziness among those who do work), then the only other means to close such gaps is through charitable donations (or other "transfer" payments) from other communities. Without such payments the gaps in inequality will persist.

If a community, however, has sufficient savings (e.g., to fund a reasonable standard of living for the elderly), then the workers production can focus on their current and future needs (and that of their children). If there are sufficient jobs, then there is a nice equilibrium with respect to prices. That is, the elderly's sensitivity to inflation eroding the purchasing power of their savings is nicely balanced with the age-based inflationary expectation of workers for increased wages.

When savings are not sufficient to fund a reasonable standard of living for the adult non-workers (that is, those who are elderly, disabled, etc.), then the current work force needs to either produce more (that is, increase the quantity of workers or the productivity of the output) or contribute more of their output to the non-workers; thereby reducing the worker's standard of living. If the able-bodied workers cannot produce more (a lack of demand) or contribute more (because their standard of living slides towards poverty), then a community becomes more and more unstable. Eventually there are no resources to take care of the elderly (and "disabled") and no jobs for the young adults. Unemployment increases among all workers and the standard of living decreases for the entire community. Children instead of falling into poverty, now begin their life in poverty.

This lack of equilibrium will continue, into perpetuity, until balance is restored with respect to the number of people, the ratio of responsible people relative to the reckless, the relationship between the producers and the consumers and a more fair allocation of the community's resources among its members.

Consider for a moment the relationship between the United States and China. The United States has a larger land mass, more renewable water resources and more arable land compared to China. Assuming similar basic consumption patterns (the median ages of both populations are comparable; China – 35.5 years; U.S. – 36.9 years), people in the United States, on average, should always enjoy a standard of living higher than China. How much greater? Well, at least 4 times greater because the United States has a population that is one-fourth the size of China. If there is no basic change in demographics, then there are only two ways for China to close this gap.

The first alternative for China is to squeeze at least four times the productivity out of the country's existing resources. Of course, this is difficult because productivity is ultimately a reflection of R~I~P~P~L~E~S. In other words, China would need to mix its R~I~P~P~L~E~S ingredients into a recipe that would be at least 4 times more potent than the United States.

The second alternative is to acquire additional natural resources and financial resources through various trade alliances. China does this by using its excess labor supply to make products others want and then uses the money that they generate to acquire and invest in the natural resources of other communities (e.g., Australia, New Zealand and various countries located on the African continent). Of course, China could also acquire additional natural resources through acts of war or from the theft of human knowledge (e.g. technology or other intellectual property).

Clearly, communities do not have to normalize standards of living in order to have a stable environment. Moreover, everyone does not need to have the same standard of living to be happy. However, if people within the community believe resources have been allocated unfairly or when entire communities believe they have been exploited for the benefit of others, then communities begin to pursue a path that often leads to instability. Many times this instability manifests itself in violence. Moreover, in an open society, where information travels freely among communities, there is an ongoing quest to equalize the standards of living in the hope such equalization optimizes each citizen's quality of life. However, because resources are not allocated equally among communities and ideology can vary tremendously with respect to how one measures "quality of life" this quest for optimal happiness will never happen.

Whether trade occurs within a community's borders or with outsiders, a community must have a standard unit of measure (i.e., currency or money) that benchmarks relative values. In most cases, especially in the richer societies, the government (usually through the auspices of a central bank) is responsible for the stability of its currency. The best way for a government to ensure this stability is to maintain control of the country's money supply through sound regulation of its banks.

Sound regulation means that its banks make good loans. When banks make bad loans, then the money supply slowly seeps into the hands of the speculators. The velocity of money slows as these nefarious manipulators gamble more among themselves and a smaller percentage of the money supply flows into the more productive endeavors that enhance output. The central banks become more chagrin as the money supply expands, growth slows and a larger percentage of the money supply moves beyond their control. In some cases, a government may use various policy gimmicks to clawback its money supply such as higher taxes, fines, penalties, assessments, judgments, and in some cases outright nationalization of the speculators' assets. The speculators, of course, will use every means possible to avoid such outcomes. The government central planners who create the money supply and the speculators who mange the flow of money in the world's trading casinos are in a constant battle for control.

As the speculators gain greater control of the money supply, the community will experience tremendous price volatility and an increased frequency of booms and busts caused by asset bubbles that typically manifest themselves in overvalued real estate and stocks. If the government's claw-back strategies do not work (which they won't), then the central bankers will increase the amount of the money supply (inject more liquidity into the system) in the hope new loans will stimulate the economy, prop up the overvalued assets and dilute the impact of the speculators. Sadly, once this cycle begins, the most likely outcome will be bouts of temporary inflation leading to more uncertainty followed by periods of massive deflation in the overvalued assets and stagnation.

As speculators circle the globe like vultures looking for wounded prey they will act as mercenaries in the currency wars that ratchet up the instability of societies. Their hope is that the velocity of money will eventually destroy the velocity of trade. They have no interest in converting their money into productive assets (buildings, factories, bridges, roads, railways) that create the jobs that produce a community's goods or provide its services. Their only interest is the arbitrage they can create between the return on a paper asset and the paper debt used to finance their paper bets. This is The Capitalist Hypocrisy.

Always remember, money is nothing more than a claim against the community that issued the currency. With respect to a country (unlike an individual or a corporation) this claim exists irrespective of whether a country's source for spending is the money that it prints or the debt that it issues. Once spent, the only way a country can bring this money back into its vaults (and reduce the money supply) is through "taxes" (which includes any form of asset confiscation from it's citizens) or the sale of public assets to private interests (privatization). However, when a country has no assets to sell (or if such assets have minimal value because they are difficult to monetize) and is not able to generate sufficient "taxes", then it is technically insolvent. In addition, countries by definition are "sovereign" and therefore creditors have no legal or enforceable right to seize assets from the government. Consequently, the insolvency will manifest itself in a declining relative value of the country's currency until it reaches a point where no one wants its money. When there is no money, there is no trade. When there is no trade, governments and economies collapse.

Whether you keep your dollar bills hidden under a mattress, stored in your local bank or invested in U.S. Treasuries, its value in the future is totally dependent on the stability of the United States. Low dependency ratios (i.e., high rates of employment coupled with optimal demographics), increasing standards of living and overall satisfaction with a reasonable quality of life are the outputs that document an optimal mix of the R~I~P~P~L~E~S forces. In the short run, these metrics can be masked by an increasing expansion in the supply of money for the sole purpose of putting people to work with little regard to the value of what the worker produces. However, in the long run, instability will ultimately show itself and when it does, the relative value of a community's currency will decline and the volatility of its prices will perpetuate the instability of the community.

Once stability is achieved it is often difficult to sustain because members of a community will always find reasons to take greater risks. This is especially true in the world of money, because stability encourages investors to add leverage for the sole purpose of enhancing returns (thereby allowing investors to keep redeploying capital even into riskier areas). Risk creates more volatility, fueling asset bubbles and the subsequent cycles of economic booms and busts.

Every community needs to define the right long-term equilibrium between its natural resources and the demographic profile of its members. An increasing population that accelerates growth to unsustainable levels will eventually be paid for with an aging population that will reduce output because of fewer workers and lower productivity. If this change is accompanied by a depletion of natural resources, then the community's standard of living and most likely its quality of life will decline.

I hope you now understand how closely interrelated and linked the forces of R~I~P~P~L~E are to a community's desire to sustain peace and stability. You will notice the relationship between a community's natural resources and its demographic profile is what shapes the initial portrait of a society. You will appreciate that sloppy projections of future demographic changes wreak havoc with a community's ability to invest in the right infrastructure. You will recognize increases in inequality among the members of a community are the sparks that ignite the flames of instability. You will grasp that uncertainty with respect to policies and prices cripple a community. You will discover leaders who don't trust the collective wisdom of their constituents condemn their people to a lifetime of misery. You will witness leaders who make promises they can't keep, resulting in endless suffering to those who trusted their advice and counsel. It will bother you that many people cannot escape their chains of heartache and grief. You will pity those communities which have the misfortune of perpetual instability so other societies can enjoy sustained stability. It will sadden you that refugees will die behind the barricades of their neighbors, begging the more fortunate to at least give their children an opportunity for a better life. Finally, in the end, you will sympathize with the limitations of the human race. You will acknowledge human nature is complex and there will always be unintended consequences from our decisions. Responsible decisions will have reckless outcomes and somehow reckless choices will end up okay.

FINAL THOUGHTS ON
R~I~P~P~L~E~S

I guess in the end I can't get away from my core training as an accountant and an auditor. I see economies from a long-term Balance Sheet perspective and not from a short-term Income Statement or profit outlook. I'm less focused on production and consumption patterns (growth defined as an increasing gross domestic product, or GDP) and more focused on the efficient use of resources that increases one's standard of living and leads to a higher quality of life. That is, a more stable and happy life.

What a community measures does matter. If the measurement is wrong then the behavior also will be wrong. "Growth" should not create more poverty than it alleviates. GDP is the wrong measurement for stability and happiness. I don't know what is the right measurement. I know it's complex.

I think ultimately the measurement should be some form of resource per capita. It should be increasing, demonstrating that both people and planet are getting healthier over time, not the opposite. A more symbiotic relationships between these two key resources. My measurement would exclude money as a metric. **Paper currencies may measure the wealth of nations, they don't measure the health of nations.** Money is a dismal way to store or assess long term value. Money perpetuates the illusion that wealth grows or evaporates based on the changing value someone assigns to a piece of paper. In the end, any measurement that is based on money only measures quantity, not quality.

The assets on my balance sheet would include all of the community's natural resources and the ability of the people to interact with each other in a manner that increases resources per capita every year. In other words, instead of a focus on mindless depletion and harvesting all of the low-hanging fruit, we would focus on how to achieve more by consuming less. Instead of jobs dependent on the natural resources we consume, employment would be driven by our ability to exchange ideas that improve our physical health and mental well being. Instead of growth being driven by more consumers consuming more stuff, we would measure growth as more people living happy and healthier lives (better families, better relationships, better people) on a healthier planet.

More people should not make our economies better off. Fewer people should not make our economies worse off. Maybe we should rejoice that women are ultimately in charge of human population trends. Each community should strive to reach a point of equilibrium where a change in a community's population would no longer impact an individual's quality of life. Our goal would be to never hit a plateau, because eventually standard of living and quality of life would no longer be dependent on the acquisition of more stuff. Instead, we would redefine wealth as what you keep, not what you spend. A new metric that captures prosperity and happiness. A way to measure whether a community is not only stronger, but whether it's strength is sustainable.

I have not come up with a way to calculate this metric. It is a project for tomorrow. However, if I were the leader of a community I would inventory my natural resources (using non-money measurements and a priority scale), compare it to the demographic profile of my people, and develop a coherent long-term vision and plan on how our community will sustain itself for generations with an improving lifestyle for most of its members. Then, depending on this assessment I would develop the strategic relationships with those communities that have similar views and complimentary resources and similar values. Perhaps a new way to do accounting, but this time with accountability.

In the future (maybe a project for my great great great great grandchildren) I believe someone will develop a comprehensive and cohesive model that embraces the forces of R~I~P~P~L~E~S. It will be a momentous task because it probably will require the skills of a particle physicist to search for those invisible forces of human nature that are difficult to shape or model but ultimately impacts how happiness evolves or explains why misery endures. As we have learned, the spark that often ignites hope is in reality the flame that will burn many in Hell.

Maybe in the end global stability is nothing but an illusion. A hope. A wish. A populist cry for salvation. Something we achieve for a brief moment in recognition that it will never endure. Like the strange subatomic B meson, maybe our world is hopelessly unstable. A world where how we measure the amount of money is the only thing that matters. A world where we watch corrupt and incompetent leaders slowing destroy every economy as the masses beg for something better. We fail to realize Mother Nature is the entity in ultimate control of the human race. However, instead of working together to achieve a better world, we battle among each other to destroy the one we have. Perhaps we are left with R~I~P~P~L~E~S reminding us human beings are either;

Responsible		**R**eckless
Individuals		**I**nsincere
Pursuing		**P**uppeteers
Policies	or	**P**romising
Like		**L**ittle
Economic		**E**xcept
Stability		**S**adness

CREATING YOUR FUTURE

WHY CAREER
MANAGEMENT IS
THE PRIMARY DRIVER
OF YOUR FINANCIAL
REWARDS

I know you can't wait to dive into the nuances of a successful investor. Well, you're almost ready; but not quite. Capital will not be a source of financial independence if you poorly manage your career. Now is the time to focus on your output and the growth of your wages. The successful management of your career, coupled with disciplined spending, are the cornerstones that build the savings that are the source for your future capital investment. In other words, career management in your 30s will create the financial capital for investment in your 40s. It's your future. Create it. Own it.

I want you to understand that during your 30s you must invest in yourself. Human capital is your most critical asset and this asset includes hundreds of skills that impact your success. This portfolio of skills must be actively managed by you which includes periodically rebalancing (no less than once every three years) to make sure your inventory of skills has the proper allocation with respect to market opportunities. Understanding how employers assess your skills and matching skills development with career opportunities is the primary purpose of this chapter. In other words, **during your 30s, there is nothing more important to your future financial independence than proactively managing your career.**

Getting to 30 divided work into two basic types of jobs — those based on performance and those based on activity. The Greatest Generation (those of my parents and grandparents) survived the Great Depression and won WW II. They participated in the birth and growth of the greatest private companies that became known as the Fortune 500. I think of them as the performance-based generation. They were focused on increasing the velocity of trade and the mobility of people. They were savers who recognized the importance of having sufficient resources to pay for a relatively comfortable retirement.

I am part of the Baby Boom Generation. Our generation spearheaded the greatest growth in entitlement programs of any generation. We are the activity-based generation. We are the spenders who focus on printing money and spinning it through an increasingly complex web of regulatory hurdles. We make promises we can't keep and are dependent on pension plans that do not have sufficient assets to meet their obligations. We take from your future so we can survive ours.

You are the Millennials. You are torn between the pull of perceived security in an activity-based job and the push to excel in a performance-based career. You recognize that wages will never be sufficient to fund an unsustainable debt-fueled lifestyle. You know the future will have few well-paying jobs and that retirement benefits will be less generous than they have been for The Greatest Generation and the Baby Boomers. It's impossible to even visualize retirement when you can barely make ends meet today. However, you still have hope because you are part of the world's first real global generation, where the Internet has fueled the age of information and the velocity of ideas. You now begin to realize financial independence is the means to true freedom. That is, only when you have sufficient resources to meet your basic needs will you have the flexibility to do what you want. To achieve this independence, then you, not others, need to take charge and create YOUR future.

As you grow older you will recognize there are essentially three different worlds that engulf most individuals. The first is the world of Make Believe where misty eyed idealists hope and pray for unrealistic scenarios. The second is the world of the Power Elite. It is unlikely you will run with this crowd in your 30s and therefore we will defer this discussion until you reach age 40. Finally we have the world of the Practical. This is your world; a world where everyday you face new opportunities and threats that enhance or diminish your path to financial independence.

In order to navigate the world of the Practical you need to understand your value to the marketplace. There are numerous ways to measure value, but one of the most common is how much money do you earn per hour of input. If we start with 8,736 hours in a year and you sleep on average one-third of this amount, then you have 5,824 hours of maximum capacity labor hours that you could use to generate income. In the United States an average worker might work 40 hours a week with a month off for vacation, holidays, sick days and other employee work benefits. In other words, an average individual would invest one-third of their waking hours (i.e., 1,920 hours) in their job. The question, of course, is how do you maximize the amount you get paid for this effort? How do you optimize your earnings potential?

HOW MUCH MONEY DO YOU MAKE TODAY?

Hard to believe. You're 30. Wow. Here's a question for you? How many hours do you invest in your job? Use the past year as a benchmark. When do you leave in the morning? When do you arrive home? How much effort do you put in during the day and on the weekend. How many hours do you take off for lunch? How many hours do you take off for vacation, holiday or sick days. In other words, how many hours do you actually work in your job. Now is the time to stop for a moment and ask yourself, "What really is my input?"

Here's the next question. What do you get paid for this effort? What is the gross pay on your pay stub plus any tax-free or tax-deferred benefits (most likely healthcare, 401K match, or employer contributions to a defined benefit pension plan)? This amount represents your total wages.

Divide your total wages by the hours you work. How much did you earn for an hour of your time? That is, what is the value of your input into your organization's economic model? The price you earn for an hour of your time is the most critical metric that measures your worth to the market place. It is the return you earn on your most precious asset, your time. Rising wages is the primary indicator your time is becoming more valuable. It is the best proxy to determine if the investment you are making in skills development is providing a reasonable return.

Value per input is your personal exchange rate and is similar to any key price metric such as the stock price for a company, the interest rate on debt or the value of a country's currency. And, as you will see, you must build skills in order to strengthen the value of your personal rate of exchange (buy my services because I deliver value) or you will be forced to reduce your wage rate because competing on price will be your only real advantage (hire me because I am cheap).

Your lifetime economic value during your years of employment is the amount of compensation you receive based on the hours you work. You need to know what this metric is today, why it reflects the number it does, and what trend line you should expect for the future.

For example, in 2014 the median income for an individual with a college bachelor degree was $48,000. If we assume such an individual worked an average of 1,920 hours (i.e., 40 hours a week for 48 weeks), then the value of their input was $25 per hour.

As a point of reference, in 2015 the U.S. Federal minimum wage was $7.25 per hour although several states and cities mandated higher amounts with Seattle topping out at $15 per hour. Minimum wage is the lowest hourly remuneration an employer can legally pay an employee for an hour of input. In the United States, individuals who are paid a minimum wage usually work in low turnover public sector jobs (e.g., federal, state or municipal governments) or in high turnover private sector jobs (e.g., fast food and retail industries). Most of these jobs require minimal skills (i.e., they are easy to learn and require little education).

Skilled based jobs may also pay a minimum wage, especially if there is a glut of qualified applicants relative to the number of jobs or the community does not place a significant value on ones particular set of skills. Like it or not, **what you learn may not reflect what you earn.**

The reason you Become Educated (Principle I of *Getting to 30*), at least from an economic perspective, is to minimize the likelihood you will work in a job that requires minimum skills and pays a minimum wage. Supporters of the minimum wage believe it increases the standard of living for all workers. It might. However, in the United States you will NEVER achieve financial independence if your sole source of income is a minimum-wage job. For the most part, single full-time workers who earn a minimum wage live in poverty.

During the next 10 years, you should measure the economic success of your career in relationship to how much you earn relative to the minimum wage. There is no absolute benchmark; except it should be a multiple that is increasing at a much faster pace than inflation. In my opinion, a reasonable benchmark is three times the highest mandated minimum wage in the country when you turn 30; and nine times when you turn 40. For example, in today's dollars (based on a standard work year of 1,920 hours) you would earn $86,400 ($45 an hour) at age 30 and $259,200 ($135 an hour) at age 40. In other words, at age 30 you should be three times more productive (with skills that are more valuable) than a minimum wage worker and at age 40 you should be nine times more productive. If you're on target, then my goal is to keep you on target. If you're not on target, then my goal is to help you get on target.

That said, one or more of you might choose a different path. That is, you may decide a particular cause (a personal passion) is more important than what the market will pay you for your skills and your time (that is, if you would have chosen a different path). There is nothing wrong with such a view. In fact, most of the observations discussed below are even more relevant if you are driven by a cause versus driven by the money. Moreover, as you will see, if you successfully convince the market the importance of your cause you might achieve the best of both worlds (enough money to live a reasonably comfortable lifestyle). If you cannot convince the market your cause has value, then you must be willing to accept a standard of living that will be less than optimal (for yourself and your family). If you move down this path, you still may be able to develop a lifestyle filled with happiness. However, to do so you must not only embrace the recommendations of this chapter, but perhaps more importantly, the ideas in the next chapter Learning To Save, will be even more critical to unlocking the door that leads financial harmony.

THE PATH TO FINANCIAL INDEPENDENCE

To achieve financial independence it is important that you are paid a value that reflects your worth to the marketplace. Whether you like it or not, how much money you make during your prime work years matter. The more it matters to you today, the less you will have to worry about money in the future. If you reach this point, then, and only then, will you have real freedom.

To understand what you are worth, you need to assess five "how" variables. How hard do you want to work, how do you measure the output from your work, how do you increase the productivity of this output, how does the market value this output and how do you enhance your value to the marketplace. Ultimately, how you answer each of these questions will depend on very specific skills.

Financial freedom is certainly relative. You could choose the lifestyle you want and seek the income to support it. Or you could choose the career you want and accept the lifestyle that it supports. Both processes have value and most people actually flow between these two alternatives as they move through jobs and careers that often extend beyond 40 years.

At 30, I hope you now understand, at least from a personal economic perspective, skills matter only if there is a market demand for those skills. You can't specialize in what you love if there is no one who values your skills. I love the sport of racquetball. It is my passion and I'm relatively good at it. In 2014, the #1 men's racquetball player in the world made $150,000 while the 10th best player barely eked out the income of a minimum wage worker. Even in 2015, at age 59, I could probably beat other highly skilled athletes, like golf great Rory McIlroy or basketball legend LeBron James, in a good game of racquetball. But, who cares? I have a skill set that has minimal value beyond its ability to entertain practically no one; except myself.

However, one market-based skill I did possess was a good understanding of mathematics and the numbers that always made the most sense to me were preceded by a dollar sign. Undergraduate business students had a choice of majors, but the most gifted students always seemed to gravitate to the more complex courses in accounting. I enjoyed the language of currencies, it was relatively easy for me to master, and therefore accounting became the foundation of my fundamental skill set.

Accounting is like all higher-level disciplines; those who don't understand it really can't appreciate its value. Most naïve individuals think of accounting as a way of recording when money flows in and flows out of an entity. Bookkeeping money flows, except in the most simple and elementary situations, never reflects what is real; what is truth. Accounting is not bookkeeping. Accounting is the science of using money to measure when transactions create or destroy value and when obligations arise or are settled. Like all sciences, there are certain rules that must be adhered to and auditing is the way to verify companies and other entities report their financial results in accordance with such rules. Auditors are essentially the referees in a game played throughout the world where players keep score with money.

As I was preparing for graduation from The Ohio State University, it was my goal to work for one of the largest accounting and auditing firms in the world. I always felt if you want to be the best, then work for the best. I mean why settle for average if you have an opportunity to become world class? In 1978, the top tier accounting firms were known as the Big 8. Accounting was a bit of a misnomer since all of the firms actually provided consulting, tax and auditing services. Today, there are only four firms (EY being one of the survivors) reflecting various mergers and the collapse of Arthur Anderson (thanks to the implosion of Enron and overzealous regulators).

The recruiting process at all of the top firms was pretty elaborate, even by today's standards. Some firms required candidates to go through various personality tests and psychological profiles while others valued in-depth personal interviews with numerous employees. I was fortunate, especially in the Midwest, that all of the firms prized hard working students who graduated at the top of their class from local state colleges versus Ivy League imports who relied more on connections and the cache of their universities. Even today, many employers still value candidates who demonstrate resilience and the ability to overcome various forms of hardship.

At 21 years old, my decision model for where I would begin my accounting career wasn't very elaborate. I had offers from all eight firms but I decided to go with the company that was founded and headquartered in Ohio. The atmosphere felt right. At the time, I just thought I was joining a large firm where I could ride the bus from my campus apartment to the offices in downtown Columbus. Little did I appreciate Ernst & Ernst (and after various mergers and rebranding today the firm just goes by EY) was one of the most highly skilled professional services organizations in the world. The sheer size of EY almost guaranteed talented individuals could find a home somewhere in the organization. It became my goal to find such a home and thus began my 20 year career at EY.

Today, EY is still ranked as one of the most attractive professional services employers in the world. For the year ended June 30, 2014, EY generated $27.4 billion in global revenues and its 190,000 employees and "shareholder" Partners represent some of the most talented men and women in the business world.

LIFE AT ERNST & YOUNG

Communities shape us and without question my years at EY influenced by views on what it takes to survive and thrive in a career. Therefore, I thought you might enjoy a short walk down memory lane and what it was like inside an organization that valued expertise and competence. So, over 35 years ago, on January 1, 1978, I began my career at EY. I learned a lot during the 20 years I worked at EY. Perhaps one of the most valuable insights was the important linkage between input (productivity) and output (value). I also found out very quickly that my most valuable education would occur after graduation from college.

In 1978, my starting salary made my eyes pop. A whopping $15,000 a year! If I worked the expected number of hours for new accountants (2,000 hours per year) I would earn $7.50 per hour (the value of my input) for my efforts. Since the federal minimum wage was $2.65 in 1978 I felt pretty good about earning 3 times this benchmark. However, at the time, I didn't understand why I earned more than the minimum wage and candidly I didn't really care. Of course, upon reflection, it was because I had obtained relatively unique skills (accounting and finance) that were in great demand in a market (Columbus, Ohio) that was growing tremendously. It was the first time I realized a growing market is what makes relevant skills even more valuable. Otherwise, in a stagnant market your only opportunity is to take a job away from someone else.

As a professional services firm, EY would bill customers for audit, tax or consulting work based on the value of its services to a client. The quality of EY's people (i.e. their depth and breadth of expertise) determined the value of these services. Value to a client was measured in many different ways. Audit services, for example, could be benchmarked to a competitive marketplace. Tax services could be benchmarked to the actual savings from an innovative solution to a complex problem. Consulting services, like Corporate Finance, could be benchmarked off the price realized in the sales process of a private company or the benefit of a lower interest rate to a client by restructuring its debt.

EY, similar to most professional services firms, requires all employees to track and record almost every hour of their professional lives. It's a mundane and tedious task. I hated it. However, early in my career this discipline was one of the keys to developing excellent organization and project management skills. That is, time tracking taught me how to meet deadlines and complete a task on budget. It's not possible for you to increase the value of your output unless you have a clear understanding where you spend your time and how you spend your time. Logging your time daily is the only way you achieve this insight.

You can't "save" time unless you understand where you spend it. Track it, analyze it and change your patterns of behavior. Covert lost productivity into more value by using your time more efficiently.

Output was measured in hours and the value of this output was measured in the amount of money the firm collected per hour. Most professional services firms (i.e. lawyers, engineers, architects, graphic designers, etc.) function under a similar business model because the primary product or service (knowledge and ideas) is delivered by an employee and the primary cost driver of the firm are the total salaries (i.e. wages and benefits) paid to its employees. What is important for you to understand is today, and in the future, your worth (and/or your Company's value), especially early in your career lifecycle, is based on a service you provide to someone in the supply chain.

Value of Output = Worth To A Stakeholder

In 1978, EY would price the value of my output at $30 per hour or approximately 4 times my starting salary. In other words, the value I brought to EY was $7.50 per hour, the perceived value to the client was $30 per hour and the difference was the money EY would used to operate its business (office rent, administrative staff, employee benefits, technology, supplies, etc.) and what was left, or profit, would go the partners, who were the owners of the Firm.

So, here is an interesting paradox. In any given year, poor performers would actually make more money than exceptional performers. How could that be? Well, there were three primary reasons. First, exceptional performers, who were consistently in higher demand, would generate more hours of billable output. Second, exceptional performers would invest more time in endeavors that would enhance their skills. Third, both performers would be paid essentially the same salary. For example, in my first year with EY I billed 2,500 hours and invested at least 500 more hours in skills enhancement and other non-billable activities (troubleshooting issues, preparing for meetings, proofreading my work, etc.) while certain peers billed 1,500 hours while enjoying a greater amount of leisure time. Do I sound jealous? Well, I was! I'm earning $5 an hour for my input while some of my peers were earning $10 an hour. Then, to make matters worse, EY made more money off of my efforts (billing the clients $75,000, paying me $15,000 and netting a cool $60 grand) while a peer with only 1,500 billable hours generated half of this amount.

Drat! Did this make any sense? Was I nuts? Should I continue to invest 3,000+ hours a year (an average of 60 hours a week) in such a career? Did I really want to work this hard when it appeared I was actually being punished for my efforts? Well, there was logic to the madness and over time I began to better understand how EY defined winning.

Here is what I learned very quickly in the early years at EY. Pedigree (college, grades, part time work, extracurricular activities, family connections, etc.) meant everything during the recruitment process. And without question, your degree was the passport that opened the door to opportunity. However, once hired, well, no one cared who your parents were, what school you attended, how terrific your grades may have been and other glowing accomplishments on your resume. In addition, on those rare occasions (because EY learned quickly the pain of departure was greater than the perceived benefit of the hire) when marginal candidates were hired because of personal relationships (their parent was a high level executive at a client) it was only a matter of time before the immature, irresponsible, unreliable, unproductive or incompetent were shown the door. Accountants certainly understand turnover only increases costs, especially when it is caused by poor recruitment decision models.

When the new recruits were all assimilated it was clear I was competing against some of the most talented accounting and business majors in the world. I felt like a scratch golfer in a world where increasing handicaps would only send you off to thrash around on the mini tours. Now it was all about execution and those four years of college became one very small historical data point that would have very little to do with my future success at EY. Learning was now a life long education process. If you were able to learn quickly, then exceptional "students" were given more responsibilities and increased compensation. Laggards were "counseled out" to pursue other endeavors. Moreover, there was always a "lag" between performance and compensation. That is, you had to demonstrate you could consistently perform at the higher level before you were rewarded with a promotion and the benefits that came with it.

In a way, I was lucky. Performance reviews after every engagement (usually from different superiors) provided continuous feedback with respect to where I fell short, met or exceeded expectations. Annual counseling sessions (and informal feedback from trusted mentors) provided additional insight on skills assessment, development goals and career opportunities. It was relatively easy to understand career paths, timelines and the skills necessary to obtain future financial and other rewards. It was only later in my career when I recognized that very few organizations actually provide insights to employees on career paths and what it takes to get from one position to another.

Not surprising, as the years passed, the gap between peers would narrow. Competition was intense and often it would be the smallest of items that would enhance one's unique brand, differentiate one individual from another and provide a competitive edge. **At the highest levels, success is sometimes achieved at the margin where the tiniest advantages make all the difference.**

One of the first competitive differentiators was passing the arduous exams to become a Certified Public Accountant (CPA). This accreditation demonstrated a base threshold of knowledge, skills and abilities in various business matters. The quicker you passed the exam, the faster opportunities could open up for you within the firm. With hindsight, it was probably one of the easiest ways for EY to document an employee's college grades reflected some level of actual technical competence. I passed all 4 parts of the exam in November of my first year (spending my "free" time in the summer cramming for the test). I just felt it was important to send an early message to the leaders at EY that I was going to make the sacrifices necessary to invest in my career and I was serious about my commitment to the Firm.

With respect to output, here's another interesting question that I pondered early in my career. Was I an exceptional performer because I was more productive, or did I just work more hours than my peers? From EY's perspective I was more productive because I was paid a fixed salary regardless of the hours I worked — which was eventually remedied several years later when new accountants were paid for overtime hours. So, if I was actually paid for the extra hours I worked, would EY still consider me to be a productive employee, or just an employee who was willing to work hard. Well, it depends.

Clearly, there is value in the employee who will work long hours to achieve outcomes that are desirable to the Firm. Value, however, is measured in results and not effort. In any performance based organization (e.g. all professional services firms) value can be achieved primarily in only two ways:

INCREASE THE VALUE OF OUTPUT

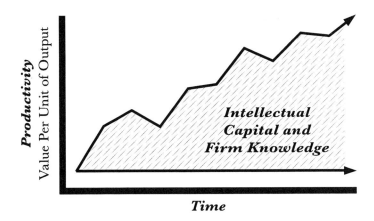

Productivity
Value Per Unit of Output

Intellectual Capital and Firm Knowledge

Time

CONTROL THE COST OF DELIVERY

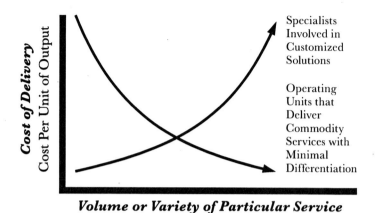

Volume or Variety of Particular Service

Organizations that want to grow rapidly will focus on the value of their output (otherwise they won't grow). Organizations that are stagnant will focus on decreasing the cost of delivering their product or service (otherwise they won't survive). Both metrics are necessary to measure productivity and both metrics working in concert are what generate the returns necessary for long term survival.

FIRM VALUE

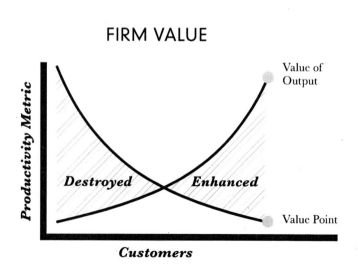

In those early days, EY could easily lower the cost of delivery by having staff members on fixed salaries work long hours. Another option, of course, is to streamline complex processes by reducing the number of steps (and often the number of people) necessary to achieve a certain outcome. However, the best option for most labor-intensive organizations is to increase the value of their output. There are two primary ways of increasing the value of your output. First, **don't give away your time for free** (e.g. not capturing or billing for client's inefficiencies that required you to spend more time than plan). Second, find ways to do things better and faster while maintaining an acceptable level of quality; productive people always learn how to be more effective and more efficient. In other words, speed was important, but like in the game of football, there was no benefit to being fast if you consistently miss the tackle.

For example, consider the following: in 1978 a typical small county hospital audit was 1,000 hours and EY received competitive fees of $30,000. If salaries are variable (that is, the cost to deliver a 1,000-hour audit is the same as an 800-hour audit) then the costs to deliver both audits were the same. The way to deliver more value to the client and to EY was to lower the hours to 800, with no decrease in quality, and receive a fee that was slightly less than our competitors. In other words, if EY charged $28,000 for an audit that we could complete in 800 hours while our competitors charged $30,000 for 1,000 hours, then our value per output would be $35 versus $30.

So we standardized processes, streamlined procedures and increased quality. As one Partner reminded me, "You can only add more customers if you continue to deliver value to the existing ones." Our competitors slowly left the industry while EY added even greater expertise. When we leveraged these synergies not only across Ohio, but then exported our K.I.T.E. (Knowledge, Insight, Technique and Experience) nationally, EY built one of the dominant healthcare practices in the 1980s. As our expertise deepened, competitors slipped to the sidelines, the value we delivered continued to increase along with profitable exponential growth.

The point is this. Productivity doesn't increase because someone decides to work more hours; even if they are compensated for this effort. Productivity increases only if you can deliver more value per unit of output and the customer recognizes and pays you (or your organization) for this effort. In other words, I can make more money (wages or W) without any increase in productivity by working more hours. There is no change in the value of my input (V_I) or the value of the firm's output. Moreover, increasing income by working more hours (H) does have its limitations since there are only so many hours in a day. In fact, most people would agree human productivity actually declines after so many hours of effort because of fatigue. As a result, working most of the day is not sustainable over long periods. In other words, **I don't want you to earn more by working more hours; I want you to earn more by working fewer hours that have greater value!**

$$W = V_I \, x \, H$$

where V_I is relatively infinite and H is bounded by fatigue

EY also taught me the tremendous impact technology had on productivity and the labor force. How do you get more output from the same input of investment and labor? In other words, with respect to output, efficient technology will always lower a company's cost of delivery. Imagine for a moment that I managed 2 employees in a small accounting firm that did somewhat complex tax returns. In one week, each employee worked 50 hours and produced 10 tax returns. The firm charged $500 per return and each employee was paid $40 per hour for their efforts. So, each return would cost $400 and $100 would accrue to the owner of the firm. Now, technology comes along and the entire process of preparing a tax return is automated and the amount of time to complete a tax return is now five hours. If the software costs $100 per return, the employee earns $200 per return, then $200 accrues to the owner of the firm. However, the real magic is 10 tax returns can now be completed by 1 employee; not 2. In other words, the decrease in the number of people is a function of the increase in productivity. That is, Technology ("T") has the following impact on productivity.

$$\% \; \Delta \; in \; Work \; Force = 1 - \frac{1}{Impact \; of \; Technology}$$

where

$$Impact \; of \; Technology = \frac{Labor \; Hours \; Before \; T}{Labor \; Hours \; After \; T}$$

Quickly I came to the following conclusions regarding technology:

- If there is no growth in output, then technology that increases productivity will always decrease the number of people in the work force. The first employees fired will always be the marginal performers, unless somehow they are part of a protected class.

- Technology is actually more like a long-term investment in infrastructure (especially if it is maintained and updated) versus the short-term cost for workers who do not update their skills and improve their productivity. People will have an increasing difficult time justifying this extra cost when technology is clearly more efficient and more productive.

- Depending on various economic forces, the value of technology will accrue principally to the supplier of the technology, the owners of the firm, the customers, and the employees who remain with the firm.

- Early adopters, close followers and others with early first-mover advantage (especially those firms that actually develop the technology) will always be in the best position to deliver the greatest value to their stakeholders. However, technology will tend to favor firms and individuals with the greatest resources because they will have the monies to develop and invest in productivity enhancement equipment and processes.

- For any organization, technology will always make sense where the cost of technology (which includes expenses related to training and a learning curve for implementation) is less than the cost of the labor it replaces. This is especially true where there are other increases in value such as greater efficiency that occurs with greater accuracy and fewer errors. For example, tax software that costs $100 and replaces $200 of labor is a relatively easy value proposition. And, as this relationship increases, it becomes harder and harder to avoid technology enhancements, especially in a competitive market.

$$Breakeven\ Multiple = \frac{Labor\ Costs\ Eliminated}{Cost\ of\ Technology\ Enhancements}$$

Ironically, technology someday will probably make the annual audit unnecessary (or certainly less valuable) for many companies. Data analytics will eventually merge the behavior, experience and background of most executives with a company's published operating results. Predictive models will credit score every company in real time and peer to peer lending will adjust the cost of capital (or the cost of credit) almost on a daily basis just like the stock market does today. Validating historical results will have minimal value when the current environment provides better insights into what is really going on in the daily activities of any company. Insurance is no longer valuable when all risks become nothing more than inputs into the total pricing process for those who seek capital and those who provide it. Annual audits may still occur, but they will probably become as trivial as the annual shareholders meeting for today's publicly traded companies.

In any event, if output at EY was measured by value, then the person who provided the greatest value to the marketplace was a Partner. Without question, Partners were accountable for the success (or failure) of the firm and Partners had the primary responsibility for relationship management with the firm's clients (and other key stake-holders). Partnership in a Big 8 firm was the ultimate brass ring in the world of accounting, especially in the eyes of a boy raised in the small towns of central Ohio. Probably, unlike many of my peers, it was my number one professional goal from the day I joined the firm. I achieved it, on October 1, 1989 and was part of the first group of partners admitted to the recently merged firms of Ernst & Whinney and Arthur Young. I was 33 years old and I had been with the Firm for a little more than eleven and a half years. Compensation? Well, it increased ten fold from the day I joined the Firm.

I spent seven years as a Partner with EY and skills development was always on my mind. For me, making Partner was not the end game. It was just one major accomplishment in my professional journey. In 1993, I left behind the role of Audit Partner and became a Partner in the Corporate Finance division. If accounting provided the historical basis for a company's financial statements, then corporate finance was the discipline that interpreted the present and unlocked the future. Corporate Finance was EY's ultimate value-based consulting service. It was one of those areas where results were 100% contingent on outcome. If you delivered, then you got paid, usually handsomely. If not, then the firm received zero dollars for your efforts. It was an important reminder that growth will not occur if you can't deliver something that adds value to the customer.

Skills provided me options and with that in mind I went back to school in 1994 (while still working at EY) and complimented my resume with a MBA from The University of Chicago. In 1996, at age 40 I left EY. It was a terrific career, but the learning curve started to feel a bit flat (things were getting a bit boring). I had a great background in a variety of industries (healthcare, retail, manufacturing, education), I had worked on small private companies and large publicly traded corporations, I had managed the IPO process for a number of our clients and assisted in the sale of companies and divisions, raising capital for new ventures and restructuring debt of troubled entities. Yes, EY, in so many ways, had prepared me well. The time had come to leverage my skills into an entrepreneurial start up. An emerging technology, in an emerging market with a new company. I was the #2 guy and was given the primary responsibility to raise $150 million to finance the company's business venture. It's a great story and I will circle back to this endeavor in a little bit.

It's hard to list all of the skills I absorbed while at EY. Without question, my mentors yanked off my plaid shirts, blue jean overhauls, white socks and boots and polished me nicely with blue pinstrip suits, cuff linked monogram white shirts, cranberry colored ties and shiny black wing tip shoes. Great mentors are like great mothers; like your

Mom! They know when to pull you forward and how to push you further.

Certainly there are the quantitative technical skills in accounting, corporate finance, taxes, valuation, investments, wealth creation, etc. However, the qualitative skills that emphasized teamwork, relationships (clients, superiors, peers and subordinates), respect, loyalty, tradition, character, ethics and community involvement were just as valuable. I strived for excellence after learning early in my career that the chase for perfection wasn't always necessary if it drove those around you (and yourself) crazy.

Of course, I learned numerous leadership skills including an understanding when it was the right time to compete, cooperate or collaborate. In the end, you learn to lead the way you were led which is why it is so important to learn from the best. I always had a pretty good sense where I was headed, what my value was in the current market, and what I needed to do to enhance my value going forward. But perhaps, most importantly, I had picked the right environment. Mentors who pulled the best out of me, nurtured me, coached me (especially those whom I eventually joined in the Partnership) and gave me the opportunity to excel.

DID I HAVE A CAREER OR JUST A JOB?

At EY I had the opportunity to observe the internal processes of many different companies that were involved in numerous industries and had a variety of different ownership structures. I gained tremendous insight during these observations including my personal view that most workers could be divided into two different and distinct categories.

Either they worked in an activity-based ("AB") job or they were trying to excel in a performance-based ("PB") career. I briefly introduced both of these terms in *Getting to 30*. However, as you begin your next decade of employment, it is vitally important you have a better understanding of each of these worker classifications. Your opportunities, your incentives, your compensation, and your future will be shaped by the category you choose or the category that chooses you.

As you read the following I want you to understand performance-based careers and activity-based jobs are not a reflection of the personal character of any individual. Good people work in both arenas. Sometimes, however, it is important to understand the extremes if you are going to appreciate the differences. However, in all situations, the attributes that define a PB or AB worker is a direct reflection of the type of organization that employs them.

A performance-based organization has the following critical attributes:

- *Outcomes are judged based on performance.*
- *Results matter.*
- *Outcomes are based on measurements.*
- *Solutions are driven by data.*
- *Measurements are linked to an entity's customers.*
- *Metrics are tangible, quantitative and objective.*
- *Key stakeholders judge an employee's effectiveness.*
- *Decision making is relatively fast but basically autocratic.*
- *Small interdisciplinary teams inspire the best solutions.*
- *Employees work the hours required to achieve outcomes.*
- *Technology that improves productivity is encouraged.*
- *Processes that reduce complexity are valued.*
- *Increases in wages are based on skills and productivity.*
- *Incentives reward meritocracy.*
- *Performance ensures job security.*
- *Value to an entity's stakeholders increase over time.*
- *Employers embrace continuous learning and change.*

In contrast, an activity-based organization has the following characteristics:

- *Outcomes are judged based on activities.*
- *Effort matters, sometimes.*
- *Outcomes are based on observations.*
- *Solutions are driven by personal opinions and biases.*
- *Measurements are linked to an employee's effort.*
- *Metrics are intangible, qualitative and subjective.*
- *Peers judge an employee's effectiveness.*
- *Decision making is painfully slow and consensual.*
- *Large redundant teams drive decision making.*
- *Employees work a designated number of hours.*
- *Technology that improves productivity is discouraged.*
- *Processes that increase complexity are rewarded.*
- *Increases in wages are based on years of service.*
- *Incentives reward mediocrity.*
- *Compliance ensures job security.*
- *Value to an entity's stakeholders decrease over time.*
- *Employers embrace ignorance and status quo.*

Many people believe performance-based careers exist only in the private sector, including most small businesses while activity-based jobs have been linked to many public sector jobs, or other organizations that are substantially funded with monies from government entities or charitable donors. In fact, one can find PB and AB workers sprinkled throughout both private and public sector employers (e.g. accountants can fit both profiles and work in either type of organization). In other words, performance driven individuals can hide within an AB organizations and task driven workers can lurk in the hierarchical bureaucracies of the most successful PB organizations. Moreover, most of us actually flow on a daily continuum between activity and performance-based events, where often times attitude is the only thing that separates us from the two domains.

THE PROFILE OF PB AND AB WORKERS

Intelligence is not what separates PB and AB workers. The most significant differentiator between these two types of workers is pure desire. PB workers take pride in their work. They want to do a good job. They strive to do things better. If they work in a PB organization they embrace the competitive nature of their environment. On the other hand, AB workers have been badgered so long by the group think of their organization that they just want to complete their tasks with minimal hassle and go home. AB workers may also love to compete. They just would prefer to compete outside of the workplace (nurturing their children in competitive endeavors; participating in various amateur sporting events). However, in all endeavors, some people want to compete for the first place trophy, others want a medal for participation and the remainder would prefer just to be left alone. Truth is, you had to compete for what you have already accomplished in life and you are going have to compete against others if you want a better tomorrow.

AB workers are relatively easy to spot and easier to complain about. It's the waitress talking among friends while you wait. It's the teacher who leaves within seconds of the final school bell. It's the seven people not working in the nine person highway construction crews as you sit in a perpetual traffic jam. It's the "help desk" that transfers your phone calls among numerous individuals. It's the executive who ties up the staff in never-ending meetings. It's the politician who speaks, but never listens. It's the lawyer who writes the laws that no one understands. It's the bureaucrats who perpetuate endless conflicts and disagreements. It's everyone who slows us down and makes our lives less efficient and more miserable.

AB organizations (or AB divisions of larger PB organizations) are also easy to identify. They are notorious for running over budget (if there is a budget), missing deadlines (if there are deadlines), and having the least effective and most dysfunctional staffs. People are hired with no idea what their superiors expect from them. Usually there is no formal process for evaluation and therefore there is no way to tell if programs, projects or processes work or don't work. Almost by design, there is a chronic failure to set priorities. If "productivity" is discussed, performance metrics (the number of meetings attended, the number of reports or papers that are written, etc.) are totally delinked from any type of customer centered measurements. That is, AB divisions define "quality" as compliance with input standards versus outputs that measure desirable outcomes. Everyone in a community's supply chain bears the cost (either directly or indirectly) of the inefficiencies embedded in their AB organizations.

Remember what we discussed earlier with respect to Leadership. How you lead depends on who you lead and the outcomes you want. Consequently, the profile of an AB leader is totally different from someone who leads a PB community. AB leaders perpetuate an illusion of improvement by constantly identifying inchoate plans that refer to change, fairness and happiness. To fire up their populist constituents, AB leaders evangelize future state scenarios that are not possible or not practical. They preach morality and a higher public calling to hide their self interests. Time becomes infinite because it is easier to deliver hope when the expectations for tomorrow will always arrive at a later date.

What is ironic, however, is that many of us would prefer the low stress of an AB job so we could spend more time enjoying those who cater to our needs from the PB workforce. The professional athletes who provide our weekend entertainment. The composers who create the music we enjoy. The storytellers who write the books we read. The producers who make the movies we watch. The designers who make the products we buy. The professors who help us learn. The physicians who treat our illnesses. The scientists who eliminate disease. The military that keeps us safe. The innovators who discover new sources of energy. The engineers who build our infrastructure. The parents who raise responsible adults. It's everyone who makes our life more enjoyable and more fulfilling.

WHO MAKES MORE — THE PB OR AB WORKER?

Well, the answer might surprise you. So, who does make the most money per unit of input? That is, who gets paid the most for the time that they invest in their job? Well, it depends.

To answer this question it's important for you to understand how wages are determined in the United States of America (which may not be the same as other countries). In other words, what are the variables that determine why you make what you make? Well, in the United States how much you earn is based on:

- Your skills relative to market demand
- Your productivity
- Your relationships
- The supply of money

In other words, the value of your input is a function of your market based skills (S), the productivity (P) of those skills, your relationships (R) and connections and the supply of money (M).

$$V_i = f (S P R M)$$

When your skills and productivity don't make a difference because

- performance doesn't matter,
- performance is difficult to measure and/or
- performance is poorly correlated with outcomes,

then your value (and more importantly, the relative value of those you compete with) is totally dependent on personal relationships and the amount of money that is available to pay your salary.

Consequently, PB organizations compensate workers primarily based on their productivity and the demand for their skills while AB organizations compensate workers primarily based on their relationships (often linked by patronage or cronyism) and the supply of money. In other words, **when performance doesn't matter the only thing that does matter are relationships.**

In an AB organization (which could be a division of a larger PB company) wages increase based on the number of years you work and inflation (the longer you work the more you earn). As a result, workers embrace pension plans that pay a retirement based on years of service and guaranteed benefits that are linked to increases in the consumer price index (defined benefit retirement plans). In addition, AB workers tend to hit their maximum salaries in their late 50s or early 60s, usually just before retirement. Of course, it's not surprising that AB workers support inflationary fiscal (higher minimum wages) and monetary (larger government deficits) policies. In other words, without inflation there would be no reason to increase wages for the average AB worker. It's probably one of the primary reasons many PB workers despise AB workers. Highly skilled PB workers understand as long as there is an adequate supply of money (taxes, monopoly rents, charitable gifts) the cost of output delivered from an AB organization will always increase, which means the recipients of such output will always pay higher prices over time.

In a PB organization wages increase because a worker delivers greater value to someone in the company's supply chain. Therefore, workers strive for structural improvements in efficiency that increase productivity. The cost of delivery this output may increase or decrease, depending on the relative value of the output to the recipient. In other words, PB workers focus on polishing and increasing the skills that the marketplace values. As productivity increases, PB workers earn greater amounts for each unit of input. That is, their time becomes more valuable, to themselves and to the market. Because compensation is tied to performance, PB workers tend to hit their peak earning years in their late 30s and early 40s.

The economic models for increasing wages in a PB career is almost the polar opposite of an AB job. PB workers understand they need to decrease the cost of delivery and/or increase the value of their output to give their organization an opportunity to grow and prosper. AB workers recognize the more they can increase the cost of delivery (more tasks) and decrease the value of their output (so there is a greater need for even more workers) the greater demand they can make for others to pay them more money (if their constituents expect any activities to be completed). That is, PB workers earn money by delivering greater value to an organization's stakeholders. AB workers make money by sustaining the status quo. It just is a totally different mindset.

Because the United States is still a meritocracy that values performance and productivity, highly skilled PB workers will make more on average than those AB workers with similar skills. In addition, as I will discuss in more detail below, the depth and breadth of skills of a PB worker will be significantly greater than an AB worker with a similar profile or job description. However, when there is an ample supply of money, AB workers with the right connections to an entrenched power elite may make more money than a PB worker who may have greater skills (especially when one factors in various tax free benefits such as employee health care and the value of future pensions).

In the United States, the best example of PB workers are professional athletes and their head coaches. Players on major team sports are usually paid based on past performance and future expectations (football, basketball, baseball, soccer and hockey) while individual athletes (golf, boxing, tennis, cycling, NASCAR, and bowling) are paid principally based on winning. The market (the number of fans and the demographic of these consumers) determines the amount of money available to pay these athletes. One could argue the skills necessary to play professional golf might be greater than professional basketball, but the reason LeBron makes 3 times what Rory made in 2014 ($21 million versus $7 million) is that LeBron's sport is more popular and entertains more people. In addition, within a particular sport (like all PB careers) the pay gap between the A performers and the other participants is often immense.

Like professional athletes, most highly skilled PB workers are paid a salary and/or bonus that is contingent upon outcomes. Compensation is not tied to the number of hours they work. On the other hand, most highly skilled AB workers are paid an hourly wage rate for each hour they work or a predefined salary that stipulates a defined number of hours they will work.

THE RISKS OF AN AB JOB

Let's take a couple of moments and review the real risks of an AB job in the most extreme scenario.

It's easy to like an AB job, especially if you have the added benefit of working in an AB organization. You probably have relatively stable pay and minimal stress because you don't work in a "competitive environment". You get up in the morning with the primary objective of showing up and leaving on time. When you physically leave the office, work is officially over, since there is a very clear delineation between work and personal time. However, while you are at work you coast or shirk your way through your day. Probably by now you've learned the shadow skills of hiding your browser history from your employer, making it easy to read the latest gossip in sports, entertainment and politics. Because your job is not demanding, you find ample time to complete your holiday shopping list, book your vacation or update your Facebook page. You might even venture into Internet porn as you frolic in the waves of cyber space. Since input is all the matters, you've mastered the art of looking busy, making excuses, and participating or organizing office meetings. In fact, you're so bored you seek out the most worthless activities just to make the day go faster. Like a computer bot, you've been programmed to mimic the performance of an actual human being; while creating the illusion you are actually doing something. You don't know what you did all day but one thing you always volunteer to others, in an exhausting tone, is "Boy was I busy today".

Maybe you've been so successful at cultivating the right relationships you actually have moved into a management position. This is especially appealing, because now you can simply delegate any real work that comes your way. In any event, you take great comfort that the lack of specific performance standards and other job security initiatives make it almost impossible to terminate you from your current position. Basically, if you're not a drug addict, criminal, terrorist or pedophile you could have a job for life.

You look at your paycheck and you think, "Ain't so bad". If you're lucky, and if you can perpetuate this charade for another 30 years, you might even have a pension that will guarantee you 100% of your then current salary for life. You rationalize your wage rate actually hits the $45 an hour target I mentioned earlier since you probably only actually "worked" 1,000 hours during the year for your $45,000 salary. I mean, what's not to like?

Of course, not all AB workers begin their careers with such cynical attitudes; many are goaded into such perspectives over time. Often they begin their job with tremendous passion and pride but when they see there is no reward or recognition for better performance they quickly slip into a daily routine of doing the same routines over and over again. When people question why they do certain things a certain way their mantra for rationalizing their performance is, "I don't

The worst place for a PB worker is trapped inside an AB organization.

know. We've always done it that way." Yet, deep down, many young AB workers actually hate their job because they know they can accomplish so much more with their life. Sadly, they've become trapped in an environment where it's easy to become lazy and complacent; silently wondering if this is all they have to look forward to for the next 30 years.

AB jobs are like that. It's not that they are bad per se but they lure you into a false sense of security that somebody will always be there to take care of you. Essentially AB workers are like a hamster, rolling around in their balls of pleasure with no direction in life. With virtually no constructive feedback on performance (positive or negative) they have no choice but to follow the AB's organization cult-like leadership model. In their belief that their jobs and incomes are stable is an underlying irony that their entire life is actually sitting on a fault line of instability. There are three major shocks that are on the horizon. The first shock is the impact of inflation; the second shock is technology; the third shock is the metamorphosis of AB jobs into PB careers.

As mentioned earlier, AB workers cheer inflation because it supports their primary argument for an increase in wages. What they fail to recognize is inflation increases the cost of everything they consume, usually at a faster rate than their wages. This increase in net inflation (relative flat real incomes and rising prices for everything else) makes it extremely difficult for many AB workers to improve their standard of living and quality of life. Moreover, when inflation manifests itself primarily in asset prices (homes and stock markets) instead of wages, it usually is the highly skilled market driven PB worker that benefits at the expense of the AB worker.

There is no doubt technology is going to continue to impact both AB and PB workers and the war for talent is going to up the minimal skill thresholds for all workers. However, it is the highly skilled PB worker who designs, builds and implements the technology and process improvements that eliminate the mundane, tedious and inefficient tasks performed by the unskilled and low skilled AB workers (and the minimally skilled PB worker). As you know, the robots you see (and the software algorithms that you don't) work 24 hours a day with minimal downtime. Although well organized AB workers will continue to advocate for regulatory and other legal barriers to protect their jobs, the relentless pull of productivity will continue to push technology into all aspects of the marketplace. Although highly skilled PB jobs eventually may be at risk (maybe someday all of us will compete against machines), it is the AB worker who faces the greatest uncertainty during the next decade. The problems are obvious when you see many workers who experience a significant amount of unproductive time, patiently waiting for some type of event to spring into action. Often they are so bored they create an event just to survive their day of drudgery.

It's scary in so many ways. In my generation, low-skilled jobs were outsourced to nations with a large population of minimally skilled workers. Your generation, the first to be totally immersed in technology, will experience the actual elimination of many minimally skilled jobs. This elimination is not only because of software and robotics. Other forces, such as online how-to video tutorials, are making it easier for people to insource tasks that used to require personal visits even from a trained professional. Society will continue to grapple with technology's costs and benefits as the number of Luddites will increase in number. However, your best defense from these unfavorable trends will be to avoid potentially dead-end occupations.

Every day we see the aftermath of worker obsolescence brought about by technology. Recently I went to a local casino to play a couple of hands of Texas Hold 'Em, the poker game. Gone were the human dealers that doled out cards, raked in the chips, paid out winnings, shuffled the deck and then repeated the process numerous times. In their place, PokerTek. A computer software program that automated the entire process on iPad screens. Sure, it took a bit of time to get use to (maybe 5 minutes), but with no chips to stack, a minimal likelihood of cheating, hands that were folded after 45 seconds with no activity, the pace of play increased substantially, providing value to both the casino and the player.

Finally, you should also consider there is a very high likelihood many AB jobs will eventually morph into a PB position or they will lose the protection of regulatory umbrellas. Everyday organizations are recognizing AB jobs are not sustainable over the long term because it becomes increasingly difficult to secure money for activities that show no results. For example, public universities like UCLA, University of Wisconsin and Arizona State University are setting aside funding for the sole purpose of commercializing promising academic research that might actually benefit society. States like Massachusetts and counties like Salt Lake in Utah are developing new financial instruments (social impact bonds or SIC) that match returns with tangible results that justify the cost of the financing.

Even traditional colleges are finally linking a student's tuition with future earnings to measure the return on the value of its education. Government entities such as the National Institute of Health and the National Science Foundation are shifting funds away from basic research to more outcome-based applied research and development projects. More pressure is going to be placed on individuals to create things that are relevant. Protected domains like medical research will focus more on actually coming up with a cure for Alzheimer's and other diseases and less on publishing, tenure and peer recognition. Like it or not, innovation will have a deadline and then money will stop flowing. You should expect these trends in the AB workplace to accelerate.

It's important for you to realize that workers who continue down this path will face a very difficult future. Even if an AB job provides reasonable wages today, it poorly prepares one for the challenges that they face in their later years. AB workers have little incentive to increase productivity when personal performance is decoupled from what they make. Protected workers have no need to modernize. Even if they do improve, progress is benchmarked off very low standards.

As you probably guessed by now, there is a significant difference with respect to how PB and AB workers see skill development. PB workers believe they must be proactive and actually create the demand for their specific sets of skills or change their skill set to match the market demand. PB workers understand they are responsible for updating their skills and educating themselves. Their goal is to develop their skills so they become more independent and therefore have greater options. AB workers, on the other hand, believe there should always be a sufficient supply of money to pay them for what they want to do; even if the work they provide is of dubious value because there is minimal or no market demand. They believe it's the responsibility of an organization to train them and expect lifetime employment as long as they remain loyal to their employer.

THE BENEFITS OF A PB CAREER

There are several obvious benefits of a performance-based job. First, because there are specific metrics to measure outcomes you receive almost immediate feedback on your performance. How your performance is assessed is the best way to understand how a performance-based company measures productivity. Feedback, of course, is how you improve your likelihood of success. Moreover, how you perform is a direct reflection on the people that manage you and consequently there are typically excellent opportunities for strong mentoring relationships with your superiors.

Of course, as you become more productive you should experience promotions that provide you fresh opportunities, as well as an increase in compensation that reflects the skills inherent in your new responsibilities. However, remember your increase in compensation may not be linear. That is, during the early years of your career (especially during your late twenties), you might actually experience a decrease in your average hourly rate as you invest your time in those activities that will make you more successful in the future (your personal investment in research and development).

Compensation, however, is not the major reason why you should pursue a PB career. The primary reason you should work in a PB job is that it will create absolutely the best environment for you to expand, polish and sharpen your skills during the next 10 years. Skills enhancement is what actually will improve your future options. Therefore, the greatest benefit of a PB career is that it provides a platform to develop and leverage a path of lifelong continuous learning. Relative to this benefit, especially during your 30s, the perceived risks of a PB career are minimal.

There is one more important reason you should work in a PB profession. It is absolutely the best career path to prepare you for an entrepreneurial endeavor. On the other hand, the novice AB worker faces a very steep learning curve if she ever decides to start her own company. In a couple of minutes, we will review why becoming an entrepreneur might be the ultimate professional end game.

SELF REFLECTION

You're 30. Guess What? Time to get serious about your career goals. The next 10 years is your decade. It will be the one period in your life when you will have the greatest mental and physical capacity for performance. Now is the time to take advantage of everything you learned during your 20s. Financial freedom is within your reach. If you are not achieving your goals, then you need to begin a process to understand why this is the case.

As you map your career choice over the next ten years, you need to be conscious of which domain you have chosen or fallen into. The two worst possible professional decisions you can make, purely with respect to compensation, are the following:

- Investing a tremendous amount of time in what you believe is a performance-based career when in fact it rewards you like an activity-based job.

- Working in an activity-based job and believing your standard of living and quality of life will actually improve from your entry-level position.

Now more than ever, you need to be keenly aware that the marketplace is becoming more and more bifurcated between lower skilled, low wage AB jobs and highly skilled, higher wage PB jobs.

So, here's the first step. Take a couple of minutes and look at your current job and assess whether it has more of the attributes of an activity-based job or a performance-based career.

If your career has more of the attributes of an AB job, then you need to be realistic about your future. As your skills become stagnant so will your opportunities. In an environment where continuous skills development is the principal path to long-term success, the eventual atrophy of your capabilities will be your demise. You will be nothing but a cheap commodity. It will be too late when you finally recognize that in tomorrow's environment, there is no job security. Eventually two things are going to happen to your AB job; Either (a) technology is going to eliminate the need for your AB position, or (b) the funding source (the money) that supports your employer will be significantly curtailed or disappear. You will wake up at 40 with no job, no skills and no hope for financial freedom.

So, if you're stuck in an AB job, what do you do? Well, you have few options. My recommendation is to use your unproductive time at work (and your personal time at home) to begin to develop the skills to transition to a PB job. This could include championing the transition of your AB job into a PB career. In the event you marry and your spouse has a PB career you should be careful not to use this as an excuse to rationalize your existence as an AB worker (principally because in the event of divorce your spouse will leave your marriage with a basket of market-based skills and you will be left with shattered dreams for your sacrifice).

If you decide you want to transition to a PB career, then you must start to think in terms of productivity. In fact, if you were sitting across from me in an interview, my first question to you would be "Do you consider yourself productive?" If you answered "Yes" (which you would; otherwise why would you be interviewing for a PB job), then my second question would be "Why? Please provide me an example of when you were productive?" If you teased me and ask for my definition of productivity, I would demur and tell you that you could define productivity anyway you want. Then, I would continue the conversation and ask you to tell me how you helped other people become more productive. When you begin to visualize productivity it forces you to think in terms of outcomes. When you think in terms of outcomes, then you begin to define quantitative and qualitative metrics that measure performance (quantity, quality, speed, certainty, risk, etc.). Trust me. It is an entirely new way of thinking for those who have been trapped in an AB mindset. For most AB workers it will be the first time that they actually start to focus on accomplishments and not activities.

As you begin to think in terms of performance it will help you focus on the times when you are most productive. Do you work better in early morning or late evening? Do you prefer quiet or chaos? Are you an introvert or extrovert? What do you really like to do? You will begin to recognize that it is your responsibility to help shape the environment that brings out the best in you.

If your job has more of the attributes of a PB career, now is the time to ask the tough questions about how you are managing your career. Do you have the right mentors? Do you work in an environment that brings out the best in you? Do you have the right skills? Are there opportunities for advancement? If you don't like the answers, now is the time to make the changes (some might even be quite radical) to your career path. Sometimes you just need to be smart enough to know where the exits are. If you're not happy with your job you need to understand why and make some changes. Every day that you don't you will become more trapped and less marketable. It's important to always be learning and growing as you look for opportunities.

You need to identify your zone of optimal performance. This zone teeters between stress (where performance targets may not be attainable) to boredom (where skills development essentially do not exist). Once you identify this zone, then you need to understand how this performance zone changes as you move up in an organization. High potential individuals are consistently functioning in the optimal zone of changing and evolving performance metrics.

OPTIMIZE PRODUCTIVITY

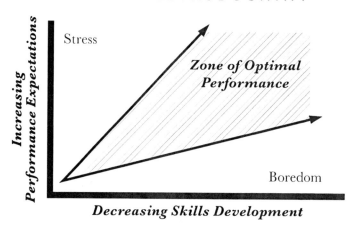

Optimal performance is achieved when talent meets great coaching. Otherwise, talent is wasted. There are lots of people who are smart or possess various mental or physical gifts. However, **without great coaching people with talent will never achieve greatness.**

Most people find it very difficult to obtain and sustain a level of optimal performance because they: (a) do a poor job identifying their real talents, (b) are unable to develop their talent because of various internal or external constraints, or (c) fail to associate with a competent coach (i.e. mentor) who can help nurture and guide them.

Great mentors are usually easy to spot (they've traveled the path that you want to take) and if you can latch on to them you've already solved one of the most important variables in your quest for success. Mentors have a natural human tendency to pick protégés who remind them of themselves which is why these relationships are so important and so valuable.

Success = Talent + Coaching

If you believe you are not achieving your optimal level of performance or if you believe you are not being fairly compensated for your efforts, the following are some questions you need to ask yourself.

Do you like the environment where you work? Is it fun? Remember, even though you might just be a cog in someone's supply chain you still should feel important and that you make a contribution. Do management, your peers and other stakeholders treat you professionally? Does the place where you work actually enhance your productivity? Or, do you waste your time on routine matters and catering to the inefficiencies of your superiors? Does your company actually care whether or not the work force is happy? Would anyone notice whether you showed up for work tomorrow? Are there opportunities for you to advance and put new skills into action? Does the company have a business model that generates an ample source of funds that is sufficient to reward its most productive workers? In other words, do you work in a culture where you feel valued and where you would like to stay?

Also, you need to be aware of the career that begins as a highly compensated PB job that slowly morphs into a highly paid AB position. There are three major signs when this occurs. First, you become bored doing the same old tasks over and over again. Second, your compensation flattens with minimal salary increases. Third, you have no opportunity for a promotion to a more challenging job unless the person you report to leaves. If this is the case, you need to recognize you are in a bad environment and now is the time to proactively seek a change.

As you know by now, my career at EY was performance-based. If you are going to be fairly compensated for your input, then you must work in a performance-based job in your 30s. The more you have direct influence over increasing the entity's value of output or decreasing its cost of delivery, the greater your relative value to the organization. For example, if you're in the "executive suite" or at least knocking on the door, then you should have such influence. The tighter this link, the greater the likelihood your compensation will reflect your performance. Otherwise, even in a PB environment, your wage increases may just barely stay ahead of inflation.

If you sincerely believe you have the right skills, but you're in a crappy environment, then you must change the environment. There is an increasing number of Internet sites and mobile apps that are designed to match disenfranchised workers with new companies (using questionnaires and algorithms like online dating services). Sites like Poacht, Switch, Jobr and Poachable now add a formal process to the informal network of professional contacts. You should expect that such sites, especially for skilled based workers, will continue to increase in depth and breadth in the future. In addition, you need to understand the jobs that the market is creating and broaden your definition of the ideal job and the ideal location. Don't handcuff yourself to a narrow view of what you might be capable of doing and where you might enjoy working. As you will recognize in a few minutes, there are many industries where skills can cross over.

As you might recall, in *Getting to 30*, Principal I was Become Educated and I used the acronym K.I.T.E. to symbolize this critical objective. K.I.T.E. represented the domains of Knowledge, Insight, Technique and Experience.

These domains incorporated the importance of becoming an avid reader, a committed listener, a keen observer and an accomplished performer. Reading, listening, watching and doing as the wings that lift the K.I.T.E. of your success.

Reading helps to give you new perspectives into today's complex world. Listening allows you to actually hear the answers to your most provocative questions. Watching is how you learn to solve problems and to do things better. Doing provides the opportunity to experiment and to refine your model for the future. With respect to career development, reading might be the most important of the four domains because it helps you to quickly filter and identify things worth listening, watching or doing. However, ultimately it is experience that provides you the wisdom that allows you to make the best decisions with respect to your life.

K.I.T.E. is how you learn - outside of the classroom! K.I.T.E. helps to ensure you maximize the value of your input by linking the right type of learning to your current and future career endeavors. It provides a platform to build your professional networks. It is perhaps the best way to allocate a person's most precious resource, that is their time.

Productivity of Your Skills $= f$ *(K.I.T.E.)*

When I look back on my eleven-year journey to Partner at EY, I sometimes wonder why I was in such demand. What I came to realize was that it wasn't so much what I did for the Firm, but more what I did for myself. Like a junkie, I craved K.I.T.E. and EY created the ideal PB environment to seek knowledge, achieve insight, use technology to improve technique and gain experience. Productivity was always the name of the game. How could we do things better, faster, more efficiently and achieve better outcomes for our clients that would translate into better outcomes for the Firm? How could we deliver more value, quicker and with greater certainty?

EY was a constant reminder that the most productive employees always sought K.I.T.E. because they understood reading, listening, watching and doing were the keys to success. Moreover, because EY was a meritocracy, the most productive employees were the ones to receive the promotions and the increased rewards that come from providing greater value to its clients and therefore to the Firm. The better employees were always involved in a process of continuous improvement because enhancing their technical, management and client relationship skills was the ticket to a promotion and, at least in my case, to an ownership position in the Firm.

In every PB organization there will always be competition, especially for the most elite positions. If you aspire to such positions then you need to have consistent performance over a long period of time (which, of course, is relative depending on the endeavor that you are pursuing). To achieve such a high level of performance you must learn to do certain things you don't like to do (cold calling prospective clients) and don't want to do (practicing a speech over and over again).

Of course, there are a couple of red flags you do need to be aware of even if you're in a PB career. For example, if you're the rare PB worker who enjoys a comfortable 40 hour work week, you still need to build future skills. If you don't spend some of your personal time keeping your skills continually up to date, you will find—because of rapid technology changes, hyper-competitive markets, and stagnant economies—that you will become the lesser skilled AB worker of the future.

Another word of caution. If you are in a performance-based job and do not see an accelerating trend in earnings and/or earnings potential, then it should elevate one, if not all, of the following concerns:

- There is minimal market demand or slowing market demand for the skills you provide in the career that you have chosen.

- There is an overabundance of supply of people who do essentially exactly what you do.

- The organization you work for does not have competent leaders, future opportunities (i.e. the company is not growing), or dedicated mentors.

- Your PB job has slowly morphed into an AB job and therefore it is more and more difficult to differentiate yourself from your peers.

- You are in the wrong geographic location.

This is why it is so important that you have a clear understanding of your real value to the market and how to capture this value. If not, then your once-promising career will devastate you, both physically and emotionally.

It is also possible your productivity potential has reached a plateau because you

- Have lost the desire to seek K.I.T.E (e.g. maybe because of family, health, religious or other reasons.

- Have not deepened the relationships with those leaders that control the access to your next opportunities.

- Have not developed the skills or a process to close the gap between what you are worth and what you get paid.

- Lack a passion for what you are doing (i.e. the career that you once looked forward to is now nothing but the daily grind of a job that you hate).

- Just don't have what it takes to be a peak performer in your chosen career.

In the event you become trapped in an AB job, or a low wage PB job, then look for other ways to increase your earnings as a part time PB independent contractor. Thanks to the Internet we are moving to an on demand economy which quickly matches an endless supply of labor and services with the needs of the market. Today, companies like Uber, TaskRabbit, Appirio, Axiom and Tongal are matching independent drivers, laborers, coders, lawyers and video makers with the market needs of a sharing economy in an age of hyper-specialization. These companies provide some interesting opportunities for those workers who prize flexibility and are self motivated, easily trainable, and have a reasonable level of C.O.O.L. skills (as defined later). It may provide you an alternative path for success. In addition, even if you don't need to pursue such a path, you should recognize that a larger share of professional capabilities are being outsourced to such companies (which is another risk to many traditional career paths).

Regardless of your current position, now is the time to take a hard look at where you are today and to determine your future career path. Clearly, massive investment that develops the wrong skills for today's market opportunities represents the K.I.T.E. that flaps endlessly in the breeze of failure. It is the demise of many highly educated individuals that wander through life with a significant amount of dead capital. During your 30s (which is now quite different compared to your late teens or twenties) learning that cannot be monetized in the foreseeable future represents nothing more than excess capacity that contributes to weak productivity and stagnant wages. Sadly, purely from an economic perspective, dead, or unproductive capital of the well-educated 30-to-40 year old, is essentially on par with the lack of K.I.T.E that represents the lost potential of the unskilled and uneducated.

SKILLS ASSESSMENT

For a period of time you might be able to ride on the K.I.T.E of others; but the most successful PB people actively manage their careers and don't passively sit back and wait for things to happen. Now is the time to take a hard look at your career which begins with a 360° external and internal review of your strengths and weaknesses with a special emphasis on the skills that will drive your future success. This assessment goes way beyond your current performance reviews. It includes candid discussions with your superiors, your subordinates, your peers, your friends, your family and other significant individuals who know you. These insights are critical because without them you're just a trapped fish, swimming around inside the shallow bowl of your perceived reality. What do others see when they look in the mirror of your reflection?

A trusted mentor and an unbiased coach can be especially helpful in this endeavor. However, beware of the advisors who have spent their entire career in the AB workplace. AB coaches are relatively easy to spot because their focus is on broad intangible performance cliches (just try harder, keep your head up, don't give up) while PB coaches are very specific on the exact skills you need to work on, or specific measurable things you need to do, in order to take your performance to a higher level. This is why it is very difficult to find a good PB coach or mentor.

Skills assessments are tricky because, like a blood test, you run a risk of identifying false positives as well as false negatives. That is, skills you think you need in the future, but you won't and skills you think you have today, but you don't. As you can tell, an unrealistic assessment can do greater harm than good. You need a clean dashboard that provides a candid assessment of your strengths and weaknesses and what it might mean to your future. There is no boiler plate model; but there are tools that can assist with this process.

Given the rapid change in many of today's industries, I know it is extremely difficult to map out years in advance a specific career path. However, understanding where you are headed and developing the proper focus on the right skills for a given career path, even if that path changes, is still important. **Now is the time to link a strategic vision with a tactical plan of execution.**

Skills you need in one career path might be totally different compared to the skills you need in another. However, what I have found is that skill sets generally can be summarized into four relevant baskets:

Critical
Concrete
Coachable
C.O.O.L.

Critical skills are those you learned in high school and include fundamental skills like reading, writing and arithmetic. They are critical because if you can't read, write or solve simple mathematical problems, then it will be extremely difficult (if not impossible) for you to develop higher level skills. Critical skills tend to measure the depth and breadth of your mental capabilities. As with most skills, a person's level of proficiency falls and fluctuates along a continuum that demonstrates a complete lack of talent and moves toward basic, advanced and expert status.

Concrete skills are an extension of one's critical skill set. In addition to higher level mental skills and analytical competence, concrete skills also include certain physical attributes. Because they are observable by all of our major senses (we can see, hear, smell, taste or feel), such skills are relatively easy to measure and identify. Generally we think of great performers in sports and entertainment as individuals who possess unique physical attributes as well as tangible technical know-how. In addition, professionals with careers in technology, engineering, art, math or science (T.E.A.M.S.) tend to have specific tangible attributes as do many vocational occupations such as welders, plumbers, and electricians.

Coachable skills are those that push or pull you to be an overachiever like eagerness to learn, willingness to work hard, ability to maintain a positive attitude and ultimately the overall desire to compete and/or cooperate. Individuals who are coachable are always seeking K.I.T.E. They are the people who have ambition, desire, focus and passion. Coachable skills are the most difficult to teach and the hardest to learn. How do you train someone to be "ambitious?" How do you teach someone to have "perseverance?" How do you learn "passion?" Why do some people seem driven and others need pushed? When talent is identical, coachable skills are what often propels an individual to the pinnacle of success. Sometimes the skills you can't see and can't measure are what ultimately separates the "winners" from the "losers".

Finally, if you are ever going to manage anyone other than yourself, then you must master the highest level skill set, which are the C.O.O.L skills. This is another acronym that stands for:

> **C**ommunication
> **O**rganization
> **O**perations
> **L**eadership

Communication includes both written, verbal and presentation skills that enhance and expand your professionalism and professional networks. Organization includes time management, self study and project management skills.

Operations include basic business acumen which requires an overall understanding of a company's economic supply chain. Operating skills could include a background in a number of functional areas including financial management, human resources, information systems, production cycles and customer relationships.

Finally, leadership includes the vision to define and articulate future outcomes and the skill to unite and persuade a large number of people to achieve such outcomes. Leadership skills include numerous characteristics and traits. For example, you need to think analytically (and rationally) to assess the pros and cons of alternative future scenarios and you must have excellent relationship management skills that help you identify the people you need to persuade and how to persuade them.

C.O.O.L skills are the most challenging to master because it requires the creativity of the artist and the attention to detail of an engineer. In most PB organizations C.O.O.L skills will always be the most valuable and once acquired, the most enduring.

Where critical and concrete skills are easy to measure, coachable and C.O.O.L. skills are generally assessed after the fact. In other words, if you're able to achieve certain performance-based outcomes (especially in more complex organizations) one generally assumes you are not only coachable but you have the proper mix of the C.O.O.L. skills necessary for success. On the other hand, if you fail, whether true or not, most people will assume your failure is because you lack passion and you're not C.O.O.L.

Your skills assessment process will include an inventory of your current skill set, a list of skills you need to develop for a future opportunity, and a gap analysis. As you can tell, there are literally thousands of skills that could be part of this assessment. Therefore, because you are running out of time to monetize your talent, it is important you choose wisely the skills that you will focus on for development. Like the great undefeated boxer Floyd Mayweather Jr., who combines the perfect blend of speed, power and technique, so must you identify and develop those skills which are critical to your success. As you go through this process, you will have to fight through any fears of failure (public speaking was never something I wanted to do) and other irrational fears (I once hated flying) that might prevent you from achieving success.

To develop and prioritize the right skills you need a system; a process. If K.I.T.E. is the HOW when it comes to developing the most productive new skills, then A.R.T. is the WHAT with respect to the skills you should develop.

Achievable
Relevant
Timely

Let's take a minute and explore each of these terms in a bit more detail.

What Skills? = f (A.R.T.)

Achievable means you have the resources to develop the skill. Most people think the primary resource is money. In fact, the most important resource for you is your time and quite candidly whether you have the raw talent and desire to develop, improve and sustain the skill. When you think of talent you need to assess where you are different and better than your peers. You're now 30. You should know what you are good at and what you really like to do. Perhaps more importantly you should have a pretty clear understanding what you don't like and what you are not good at. In addition to the feedback you receive from others there are numerous tools (personality assessments and career surveys) that can help you with this process.

When I was in my mid 40s, I thought it might be nice to become a professional golfer in time to join the senior golf tour when I turned 50. I naively believed because I had enough money for world class lessons that I could develop the necessary skills to achieve this outcome. Truth was that I totally underestimated the raw talent and all the unique skills (and other personal sacrifices) required to be a professional golfer on the senior tour. The skills gap was so vast, and the fundamental talent so lacking, that no amount of time would help me achieve this dream. Fortunately I recognized, before my investment became too steep, that I was never going to be able to swing a golf club correctly on a consistent basis. Everyone is a prodigy in something. Now is the time to truly understand where you have exceptional qualities and abilities.

Relevant means there is, or you can create, some type of market demand for the skills you have or intend to develop. In other words, of the thousands of skills you could develop, relevant means your focus is on the right skills. You need to go through an iterative process that matches career with skills and skills with career to determine your most optimal path to success. Then, once you have a match, dig deeper to identify those handful of skills and abilities that are critical to your success.

As part of this process, it's important you match your objectives with realistic and specific performance-based market opportunities. There will always be risks, unknowns and various black swan events. Nevertheless, an educated guess of current and future opportunities that match your skills will always be better than no guess at all. As part of this process, **never underestimate your ability to actually shape your future opportunities.**

In 2015, the digital economy is exploding. The "Internet of Everything" is coming with sensors capturing data about almost anything and analytics explaining how such data brings value to someone. Your skills must transition as the market changes; locking yourself into routines that cause you to keep doing the same old things over and over is a recipe for failure.

Unless you lock yourself away in a one-person activity-based pod, C.O.O.L skills will always be relevant and therefore you should always be adding to this basket of skills. Coachable skills, on the other hand, become relevant only if you enjoy your chosen career path. That is, it's difficult to have passion and drive for something you just hate doing.

In today's marketplace, concrete skills are the most difficult to assess with respect to tomorrow's market demand. On one hand, large corporations may provide tremendous opportunities for career advancement and yet on the other hand your position could be outsourced to a speciality firm or eliminated entirely by technology. Smaller organizations, especially those that are stagnant or not growing, provide even greater risks for an employee. Consequently, with respect to all skills, but especially concrete skills, you need to be performing your skills assessment no less than once every three years. At this time you need to reassess your career path based on market opportunities and adjust accordingly. What you will find is that many of the **technical skills you once valued will no longer be relevant; and if you don't develop new skills you can use in the future, then you won't be relevant.** Sometimes old irrelevant skills just need to be tossed into the trash bin of progress.

I remember when Microsoft Excel debuted in the late 1980s. Because I had recently made Partner with EY, my skills development was primarily focused on enhancing my C.O.O.L skill set, since any need I had for concrete work could easily be delegated (in fact, it should be delegated) to subordinates. However, on my own, I learned to build spreadsheets in Excel, some quite elaborate, principally because I felt the need to embrace and understand at a deeper level new technology that would be driving increases in future productivity of our workforce. Little did I know this skill set would prove invaluable years later when I left EY for a new start up. I built the spreadsheet that supported the financial model that was used to secure the financing for our company. My point is this. You need to embrace technology (maybe even develop the technology) that increases your personal productivity and your organization's performance.

Your ongoing challenge will be whether you go wide or go deep. Depending on your particular career path and personal profile it might be better to be the generalist or the specialist. Personally, I believe the generalists with a wide range of relevant skills in several areas (e.g. accounting, finance, investments, taxes, insurance, etc.) provides greater utility in today's environment versus the specialists who master one particular talent. Moreover, many individuals actually transition over time from a specialist to more of a generalist especially as he or she moves up the management ranks and becomes more of a coach or enabler of positive behaviors.

Perhaps the person with the greatest flexibility is the one who has a broad range of capabilities but if the need arises can go in depth into a number of relevant subject matters. It's a bit like racquetball and golf where certain skills like balance, core strength, and mental toughness translate well between the two sports. It's the ability to change the pitch of your K.I.T.E string between the macro and micro as you traverse a changing and volatile climate.

Timely means there is some sense of urgency and self-imposed deadlines with respect to the skills you want to develop. The skills you decide to develop might be achievable and relevant, but if your timetable is not realistic, or if you delay the development of important skills, then the opportunities to use them might vaporize. In addition, as you get older, it will become more and more difficult to master certain skills because you won't have enough time to execute the necessary repetitions to achieve expert status.

The author Malcolm Gladwell popularized a view that to become outstanding in any particular career you needed to devote approximately 10,000 hours of effort to your endeavor. Based on my experience this is a relatively good benchmark. However, this is only an average. Gifted individuals might achieve expert status quicker; less gifted individuals may never achieve such a level of expertise. Moreover, technology is going to continue to flatten the learning curve for every endeavor. Today's 10,000 hour threshold might take only 5,000 hours tomorrow. The better you understand your strengths and limitations the greater the likelihood your skills development timetable will be realistic.

Motivation will ultimately drive you to improve and get better. However, the longer you wait to identify and develop the skills you need, the greater the barriers will be to your future success.

In your 20s you might have used your diploma and other credentials to open the doors of opportunities. Not today. Performance-based organizations want tangible examples and specificity in support of representations you make with respect to outcomes. Now is the time when you begin to replace the initials that follow your name and the resumes that list your accomplishments with a list of credible personal references who can vouch for things you've done and can confirm your personal characteristics.

I personally believe everyone can be an expert in something that someone else values. Your challenge is to find this niche for yourself, refine it and build a sustainable model of productivity that works today and can evolve in an ever changing market. Visualize future heuristic models of yourself. Build a template for your virtual world of tomorrow. An Avatar that shows Model 2.0 at 20; 3.0 at 30; 4.0 at 40. How do you want the market to look at you in the future? How should you reinvent yourself? How do you monitor, analyze and reconfigure yourself to take maximum advantage of an ever changing workplace ecosystem? How do you reboot and reprogram? What really is your most efficient path to future success?

Instead of becoming a brand, visualize yourself with the features of a high performance luxury good. Someone who confers status, quality, rarity, authenticity, exclusivity and value. Visualize polishing yourself to a high sheen, instead of slopping through the marketplace with other dull commodities. Become the Porsche, Lamborghini, or Ferrari of your profession or chosen endeavor. Show the market you are the hidden gem, ready to shine.

Developing your skills is always a process of leveraging your strengths and polishing up your deficiencies. If you have a skills gap in a particular area, then you need to identify, develop, and continuously enhance the specific skill set that drives superior performance in your chosen career. The benefit you have today (which also benefits your competitors and your peers) is that there is a plethora of Internet resources that will teach you new skills, and many of these resources are free or of nominal cost. Coursera, University of the People, Kaplan, Apollo, Edx the Kahn Institute and a host of new start-ups are actively marketing training that is focused exclusively on improving specific job skills in a minimal amount of time. The content is there and I know some of you have already taken advantage of it.

Polishing practical skills, acquiring new skills, pruning existing skills and jettisoning useless skills will increase the likelihood your career path will sustain you into your 40s and 50s. Skills are like apps in your smartphone. Delete the ones you don't like and add new ones that increase utility. Change your preferences to those that truly add value. Focus.

Skills acquisition is so critical in your 30s that you should devote approximately 25% of your "work" hours to this endeavor. The amount you "work" in your job and the amount of time you "work" to develop additional skills and polish existing skills outside of your job will blur. When you like what you do and who you work with it is easier to merge your "work" hours and your "leisure" hours. PB workers are especially adept mastering this art of synergy. The "pleasure" books I read (or the audio tapes I listened to) were always related to skills I wanted to develop (leadership skills, for example) or knowledge I wanted to acquire. Building relationships with clients and co-workers never seemed like "work" when we attended various fundraising events or enjoyed weekend outings together. Some of the greatest advice I ever received was outside of "work," having a leisurely drink in a bar and merging the conversations of "work" and "life." When you are a sponge for knowledge you tend to ask a lot of questions and then spend your time listening to those who are willing to give you their insight.

The point is this. If you "punch a clock" and book your 40-hour work week and do nothing to further enhance your skills your career path will stagnate certainly at age 40 if not before. If you "punch a clock" and continuously book a 56-hour work week leaving no time for further skills development, then you run a similar risk. The only way this risk can be mitigated is if you are moving through a rapid period of skills development in your present job. Remember, many employers will exploit unskilled AB and low-skilled PB workers. However, it is often the highly skilled PB workaholic that is the easiest to exploit. Don't be a hamster, spinning endlessly on a wheel of failure.

As you pass through your 30s and approach age 40, then your skills should begin to mature (the learning curve decelerates) and you should see a relatively rapid acceleration of your earnings potential. Of course, some individuals experience this much earlier in their life cycle (entertainers such as professional athletes, singers, etc.) while others experience it much later in their life cycles (entrepreneurs, lobbyists, artists, etc.). As time marches on, your goal is to become more wise; allowing you to see problems from multiple perspectives and to understand the sensitivity of how human networks interact. The Experience piece of K.I.T.E will now become your most powerful attribute as patterns become clearer and right decisions crystalize quicker.

Remember, your only hope of achieving this result is if the value of your output is in excess of what you are paid for your input. That is, you will not move from $25 per hour to $135 per hour in a ten year period unless you understand why you are worth this amount to your organization and why your value to the market must be greater than this amount.

You cannot be oblivious to the relationship between what you are paid and how your organization, and its constituents, benefit from your employment. The more you have this understanding, the greater the likelihood that your earnings will increase and, as a result, you will capture the value you deserve. A manufacturing company that makes widgets can easily identify which employee produces more output. It's much more difficult to link productivity to performance in a service organization. EY's model that calculates value per output, I believe, is the best metric. Your goal, of course, is to capture your share of this price in a manner that reasonably compensates you for the value of your input.

You will find most jobs contain attributes of both performance-based jobs and activity-based jobs. However, your real growth (after adjusted for the impact of inflation) in wages can only occur if your output provides greater value (that is, you are productive).

$$Productivity = f \ (Skills, \ Value \ of \ Your \ Output)$$

You can only become more productive if you develop the right skills that match the profile of your changing career path. Without such an increase in productivity you run a great risk that your natural human tendencies will be to consume more than you produce, which can only be financed through debt. It is this type of debt that can never be repaid.

In summary, during your 30s you only have two choices with respect to career management: (a) develop (or continue to develop) skills that are in demand in today's and tomorrow's world or (b) create the demand for the skills that you already possess. Otherwise, you may wake up at age 40, still stuck in a worthless job (assuming you have a job) that will perpetuate lifelong poverty.

You cannot control the tides of history, but your relentless pursuit of new skills will provide you the best opportunity to surf what is going to be a volatile sea. Now is the time to map your skills with the needs of tomorrow's marketplace; coupled with a reason-

You must use K.I.T.E. and A.R.T. to optimize learning.

able assessment of your location preferences. You must have a vision of where you're headed and a plan on how to get there. Use A.R.T. to help you define where you want to go and use K.I.T.E. to help you get there. Together, both processes will give you the flexibility necessary to accelerate your career.

Career acceleration measures the rate your skills change over time in a manner that achieves the greatest success. On several occasions I mentioned the T in K.I.T.E. which refers to the use of technology to improve technique as well as your other skills. You must embrace technology within your organization and use technology to optimize learning. Time to market (meaning when you go "live" with your new or improved skills) is critically important to your success. Smartphones and their apps are one example of how machines with faster processes are merging with smarter algorithms to solve and tackle some of life's most complex challenges. Although society may still be a long way from artificial intelligence, technology that enhances your ability and increases your productivity is accelerating and you need to accelerate with it.

$$Career\ Acceleration = \frac{\Delta\ in\ skills}{\Delta\ in\ time}$$

In summary, if you're poor at A.R.T. and if you don't seek K.I.T.E. then your productivity will decline, your performance will suffer and you will sit in the parking lot of failure while others are breezing down the Autobahn of success.

So, let's look at one of the best ways to marry the skills you possess with the passion of doing things that you love.

DO YOU WANT TO BE
AN ENTREPRENEUR?

For many individuals being an entrepreneur sounds glamorous. Truth is, you will probably work harder than you ever imagined. There will be minimal delineation between your professional and personal lives. Your stress level will increase. You will feel overwhelmed most of the time. However, if you have actively built a PB career you will be in an excellent position to assess the risks of starting your own business and succeeding where others fail.

Now is the time (if you haven't done so all ready), at age 30, when you should begin to think about the problems you want to solve and the businesses you want to build. Write your ideas in a notebook, clip articles and put them in an ordinary shoe box, or document your thoughts in a digital file. Now is the time to flatten what is traditionally a steep learning curve. Just having an entrepreneurial mindset will provide benefits to you when phrases like customer solutions, performance metrics, value propositions and mission statements take on greater meaning and importance.

Trust me. You do want to be an entrepreneur. Why? Because if you begin planning today it will provide you options for tomorrow. Perhaps you want to exit the once exciting PB career that has evolved into a boring AB job where you feel you are the only one awake in a crowd of sleepwalkers. Maybe you will want to lead because you are tired of following those of lesser talents. You may want to test the ultimate skill of visualizing and articulating outcomes and then orchestrating the behaviors that achieve those dreams. Ultimately it may be as simple as feeling that you finally control your destiny (success or failure). However, even if you don't become an entrepreneur, if you begin to think like one it will do wonders for your career.

The other reason you should consider becoming an entrepreneur is that it might be the best way to earn maximum value for your real talent. What I mean is there is a wide range of income disparity with respect to the annual wages and potential lifetime earnings of college graduates (even greater for those who only have a high school degree). For example, over a career the median value of an undergraduate with an engineering degree is almost twice that of someone with a degree in art. In addition, lifetime earnings for graduates at the 90th percentile of the median are nearly three times greater than those at the 10th percentile (often reflecting the difference between those graduates who choose a PB career versus an AB job). When you start to think about what you are good at, coupled with market caps on your "career" income potential, becoming an entrepreneur might be the best way (maybe the only way) to capitalize on your current skills and those that you wish to develop.

As part of the entrepreneurial process, you need to develop an early warning system (career radar) that benchmarks your beliefs against actual trends in the industries you like and your personal core competencies. This radar is critical to your current skills development since it will help you understand and even shape the performance metrics in your current career. It's important you have a process to identify strategic opportunities. Moreover it will allow you to better assess the right time to jettison your current job and enter the doorway to a brighter tomorrow. **If you don't decide your fate, then others will decide it for you.**

Performing at the highest level is hard work. Building a company and your brand is even harder. It will be exhausting and at times overwhelming. Don't give up.

My opportunity came at age 40 during the winter of 1996. A new start-up with a license to build high speed fiber optic networks in South America. I knew nothing about telecommunications and even less about the Spanish-speaking nations of Chile, Colombia and Peru. Many of my peers at EY thought I was out of my mind, which in an odd way only made me feel better about the decision. Okay, so what if Peru, our major market opportunity, was controlled by a Marxist-Leninist terrorist organization called Sendero Luminoso, or Shining Path, just five short years ago and that the President of Colombia, Andres Pastrana was in ongoing and active peace negotiations with the Revolutionary Armed Forces of Colombia. Maybe they were right — it would be impossible to build a publicly held U.S. company, that had to comply with the Foreign Corrupt Practices Act, in countries rife with corruption. However, sometimes things just feel right and this was one of those times. Most importantly, things felt right because I had a strong belief that I had the right partner.

Patricio, the leader of this new venture, was a native of Chile. He had the technical engineering wizardry, the clarity of vision and previous success in the international telecommunications market. He had a smile that could charm the most pessimistic of naysayers and a tongue that could shatter the most confident of fools. A perfect blend of chutzpa and charisma.

I understood business models, finance, valuations, budgets and cash. I had the management pedigree and market credibility of a EY Partner. We both had MBAs from The University of Chicago to match our impeccable character and professional reputations. However, more importantly we had a certain chemistry and together, just the two of us, we raised $150 million with nothing but a License, a spreadsheet, our resumes and a business plan that injected a new technology into an environment that had the opportunity for massive scale and long term sustainability. Our horse was a stallion and we were the jockeys. In many ways we were perfect complements. Optimism and pessimism would fill our wine glasses and the blend would give us balance in a volatile market.

With a sense of urgency we closed the financing one day before the Asian Financial Crisis tanked the United States equity and foreign debt markets on October 27, 1997, (which essentially closed all emerging market financings for the next six months) and sadly, and ironically, one day after my beloved Cleveland Indians lost to the Florida Marlins in extra innings in Game 7 of the World Series. Sometimes good and bad karma can co-exist.

A formal decision model would tell almost any rational person that tossing away a 20-year career with EY to build this new company was a no go; but I had this gut feeling; time helps you with that; K.I.T.E. helps you with that. My peers didn't understand I was chasing an ideology that reflected a lifestyle I wanted to live. A belief that working in an emerging market, with a new technology and an early stage company would give me even greater options five years from now. It wasn't important for me to define those options in 1997. It was only important to know that they would evolve and I would do my best to take advantage of them. **Asking yourself what are you qualified to do today is the wrong question. The right question is, "What do you want to be qualified to do tomorrow?"** and then develop a process that puts you on a path that will eventually help you achieve that vision.

Always remember, the best learning occurs when you take a giant leap out of your comfort zone. Sometimes you have to grab the learning curve of K.I.T.E., hang on to the tail of opportunity and trust where the winds will blow you. Did I know exactly what the heck I was doing? No, not really. But once in awhile you need the personal confidence to take a game-changing shot. So, I took it.

I also had what many professionals do not. I had the support of my spouse and family. The stronger the bonds in your personal life, the better your performance will be in your professional life. I had savings, because our family lived a lifestyle that valued flexibility more than consumption. I was mobile, because I knew it might take forever for an opportunity to come to me. You have a tremendous benefit of living in the largest entrepreneurial marketplace in the world. However, if you become stuck to a location you could easily lose this benefit. Even in our global digital marketplace you still may need to physically move to match your most valuable skills to the needs of a local market. Especially in your 30s, one of your greatest assets is your ability to stay mobile.

Between now and age 40 put your ideas in that shoe box. Write them in a notebook. Expand your skills. Build your professional networks and relationships. Understand that you have accumulated a tremendous amount of information during the past 30 years and that during the next ten you will continue to generate a treasure trove of data that is valuable to someone. Your goal is to monetize this information and data; that is, monetize your K.I.T.E. Your mother suggested expanding K.I.T.E. to now include the power of your social networks (so K.I.T.E. becomes K.I.T.E.N.) Hmmm. Okay. But let the K.I.T.E.N. evolve into a crafty and aggressive adult (maybe a Tiger, Jaguar, Leopard or Cheetah).

Don't buy into the hype that only twenty something college dropouts like Gates, Jobs or Zuckerberg are successful. Truth is, most new businesses fail — for a variety of reasons. Many fail because AB workers try to leap into a world that is totally foreign to them. Others fail because the "leader" didn't have the depth and breadth of resources necessary to drive their venture to success (including basic skills in financial literacy). Some fail because of poor chemistry among the key members of the team. My hope is that success will define your legacy; not failure.

If you want to avoid hauling an elephant up a mountain, better to have a skills wheelbarrow full of powerful tools. Read and study the career path of multi-talented creative people like Okwui Enwezor (art), Pharrell Williams (music), Christopher Nolan (movies) and Phil Suarez (restaurants). They understand superior performance is what makes their personal brand appealing and unique. You're ready when you recognize the skills necessary to become a successful entrepreneur are not much different than the process you used to become a top performer in your given occupation. You will know when the time is right and when it is …. take the shot!

However, before you take the shot make sure you ask three very critical questions:

- Who, specifically, is my customer?
- What is my value proposition to that customer?
- Does that customer have enough money to pay for the product or service?

When I think of customers I wonder what exactly is the profile of the 10% to 20% of customers who actually generate between 80% and 90% of a company's revenues. How do we separate the whales from the minnows? When I think of relationships I return to what I learned when I worked with clients at EY. Some customer relationships are high touch while others are low touch.

High-touch relationships are those where you have special skills and talents that a customer deeply values. For example, many one-on-one customer relationships are high touch. Most professional services are high touch. In other words, if the personal relationship breaks down, usually because of a lack of trust, then the parties also sever the professional relationship.

The value you will get paid by each customer will depend on how unique your service is relative to the customer's ability to pay. Some of these careers deliver a high value per output, for example powerful brokers (investment bankers, real estate agents, lobbyists and art liaisons) professional advisors (lawyers, accountants and wealth managers) and providers of professional services (architects, engineers and physicians) while others deliver a lower value per output, such as barbers and personal trainers. If your entrepreneurial business model is based on delivering high touch professional services, then the only way to increase the value of your input is to move up the value chain. The way you move up the value chain is to enhance your skills and/or deliver your services to higher net worth clients (those that have more money). For example, a surgeon's value is greater than a family physician and a personal trainer of professional athletes is more valuable than comparable individuals who are training high school students. High touch professionals can also move up the value chain with scale (adding more customers or increasing the number of customer interactions) but such a model usually requires the company founder to be more involved in management and less responsible for direct customer service delivery.

Let's look at two examples of high touch professions. My barber charges $25 for the 30 minutes it takes to cut my hair. My surgeon charges $1,000 for the 30 minutes it takes to perform my colonoscopy. Both relationships are important to me; but the relative value of my surgeon is 40 times more valuable than my barber. If we assume both individuals have reached maximum value for their profession, then the only way for either individual can earn more money is to move into management and leverage their expertise among similar providers. That is, open a beauty salon or a surgery center.

Now, on the other hand, low-touch relationships are those where there is virtually no interaction between you and those who consume your product or service. The customer experience is still critical, but this experience has virtually nothing to do with a customer developing a level of personal trust directly with you. In these situations, first mover advantage and scale are everything and therefore execution to achieve this scale is the overall key to success. For example, technology companies (Apple, Amazon, Google, Facebook, Twitter, etc.) and most app developers have low-touch customer relationships. Professional entertainers (i.e. actors, musicians, athletes, etc.) would also fall into this basket because the individuals who design the products or deliver the services have no direct one-on-one relationship with their customers. In such endeavors scale and leverage is how you maximize the value of your input once you design a product or service that a customer values.

As you probably guessed, scale and leverage is critical to building most successful entrepreneurial businesses. You should not confuse such an endeavor with the millions of small businesses which are essentially nothing more than lifestyle choices. Many of these are just glorified hobbies that usually do a poor attempt matching what someone likes to do for pure pleasure with a real market demand. It is one of many reasons why small businesses have such a high failure rate. Of course, there is nothing inherently wrong with a small business lifestyle venture and some do, in fact, succeed. However, if you are a top-tier employee in a world class performance-based organization, it is unlikely you will increase the value of your input by starting your own small business. I might have enjoyed the independence and freedom of hanging my own shingle for DGG II Accountants, but the financial rewards would pale in comparison to my skill development opportunities and earnings potential at EY.

Therefore, from a customer perspective, the best entrepreneurial opportunities are those that provide greater linkage (more value to a customer) and/or leverage (more customers). In all situations, new customers expect you to provide a better solution to a problem. Problems usually exist because products and/or services are not fast, not secure, not safe, not healthy, not cheap, not fun, not entertaining, not helpful, etc. Problems exist because people have excess capacity or too much stuff (Uber: cars; Airbnb: homes; Ebay: goods). However, as inventors rush to make dumb devices smart (put a chip in it), be careful you don't become one of the many who oversell the benefit of the problem you are trying to address.

Grab your smartphone for a moment. Look at all of the apps on your phone. Every app is a business for someone. Think of the apps that you use and why. Think of the ones who don't use and why not. Which apps did you pay for? How did you pay for them? Which ones were "free"? How would the owner of each app describe you as a customer? What about the infrastructure behind the app (the owner, employees and independent contractors)? How many paying customers do they need (or advertising dollars) to break even based on specific price points? How many of these apps probably won't be on your smartphone a year from now? Why is that? If I was teaching a course for entrepreneurs I would probably ask my students to turn on their smartphones and begin to visualize and dissect the business models for each app.

As we move more to a "concierge" economy, think of how you could run your entire company with a smartphone of apps. In fact, you could build a fundamental platform for any website in a couple of hours using services provided by Wix, Weebly, Jimdo, Squarespace and WordPress.

With respect to design, think of a product or service that anchors an annuity:

Blade	→	Razor
Fiber Optics	→	Data
Tax Perparation	→	Audit Services
iPhone	→	App Store

You get the picture. Make sure you can define the specific value proposition to the customer and that you link the key performance metrics of your company to this value proposition. Remember, it's how the customer defines value; not how you define it. Use R~I~P~P~L~E~S to map the social-economic landscape and to better understand where your price fits in the overall value chain. Stay focus. Always consider that the most innovative ideas will disrupt traditional business models.

There is one entrepreneurial endeavor that requires no interaction with any customers: the life of a professional gambler or financial speculator (really there is no difference between the two). Essentially you win if someone else loses. That is, the value of your output goes up as long as the value of your opponent's output goes down. The best gamblers always pursue K.I.T.E. because their goal is to remove luck, reduce uncertainty and eliminate randomness in the hope they can create consistent positive outcomes. I know many individuals would not consider this an entrepreneurial activity. However, most would agree it is probably one of the riskiest of all of the performance-based careers.

Fortunately, you are entering your primary years of professional growth when entrepreneurship is going though a massive period of democratization. Web sites like Edison Nation, Quirky, Innocentive, Kaggle, Idealot and Ideapod provide platforms to allow your ideas to be critiqued by experts and other users. Startup hubs, tech accelerators, and new franchises are springing up throughout the nation. Consumer goods, especially, are increasingly being financed by new innovative crowd funding sources of capital such as Kickstarter, and Indiegogo. Peer to peer lending is increasing rapidly with Lending Club, LendingTree, OnDeck Capital and Prosper working to match those who need capital with those who have money to lend.

More and more universities are setting aside venture capital monies to fund startup companies to commercialize research that is being conducted by its faculty and students. Philanthropic organizations, like the Bill & Melinda Gates Foundation, are investing significant funds to solve the world's most pressing health and social problems.

If you take time to build a good performance-based business model (with relatively easy to understand breakeven points and payback periods) there is a very good chance you will find the capital to fund your passion and the mentors to help bring your ideas to reality. You should be cautious about trying to bootstrap a new company solely with your personal funds. It's important to have a realistic level of working capital and outside investors will have connections that can open multiple doors of opportunity. Start-ups fail for a variety of reasons; lack of money and poor professional networks are often the primary cause of such failures.

You are fortunate to live in the vast United States, a culture that still embraces entrepreneurs. In a relative sense, regulatory red tape (incorporation and any required permits) to form your business is minimal in most states. If things go wrong, bankruptcy laws provide the flexibility of a fresh start without the stigma of failure. Hiring and firing of employees is essentially painless (at least from a regulatory perspective). In other words, relative at least to other countries, most of the barriers to your success are internal (do you have a product or service that has a market demand) and not external (regulations that stifle private enterprise).

As you build these business models, stay virtual. Outsource non critical functions and minimize fixed costs. Remember, the best commercial ideas always make money, eventually, and the best charitable ideas always solve some type of problem. Don't underestimate the importance of cash. Whatever cash you think you need prior to breakeven, double it! Prototype development and demand creation is more expensive than most people think. Validate your prototype by finding at least one customer that is willing to use your product or service.

Keep your core team number small. Two; no more than five. You don't have to be #1, but you must be in the executive suite, a critical member of the team and an equity participant. Develop and listen to a Board of seasoned advisors. Skills should complement; not duplicate. Chemistry is important but it should be clear who will make the tie-breaking decisions. You must be able to convince investors you can create value via effective execution.

Be realistic in calculating your opportunity cost of capital. I took a significant pay cut (initially) when I left EY. No entrepreneurial start up venture is going to compensate you the market value of your talent. Why? Because value of input is tied directly to the value of output and quite candidly, you can't demand value for something that doesn't exist. Therefore, you must have enough confidence that (a) you will achieve the desired results or (b) your experience will increase your value per input for your next career move. However, if you do achieve the desired results, then the value you receive should correlate with the value you create. In other words, if you're willing to take the risk, then you should share in the rewards of a successful outcome. A successful start-up venture is actually one of the few ways to discover the optimal monetary value of your talents in a meritocracy.

Finally, start to think of yourself as an entity that absorbs, creates, and produces intellectual data. This data is powerful and has value to many entities. Your challenge will be how to capture, store, analyze, distill and ultimately communicate this information. Once you truly understand the algorithms of value you can move forward with an active process to leverage and monetize your personal K.I.T.E. In closing, there are tremendous rewards (personal, financial and otherwise) in launching and steering a venture to success. Keep looking for those opportunities and when the time is right, take the shot.

SUMMARY COMMENTS FOR CAREER MANAGEMENT

During your 30s there is an optimal mix of skills that offers the highest expected wage rate per hour for a defined level of risk. Risk manifests itself in a number of different ways including an understanding of what skills you should develop (A.R.T.) and how to develop those skills (K.I.T.E.). What makes for the most efficient portfolio of skills is doing what you love that provides the greatest return. I call this the Efficient Skills Frontier.

OPTIMIZE SKILLS PORTFOLIO

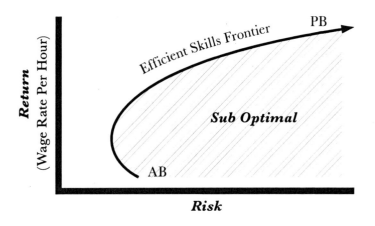

Baskets of skills that lie below the Efficient Skills Frontier are sub-optimal because they do not provide enough return for a given level of risk (e.g., being stuck in a minimum wage AB job). Baskets of skills that cluster to the right of the skills frontier are also sub-optimal because they have a higher level of risk for a defined rate of return (e.g., a PB job where what you earn is 100% contingent on performance).

One of the reason the skills frontier is curved, rather than linear is in recognition that there is a proper mix of skills and PB/AB characteristics that define a person's perfect job. Because of their youth, Millennials should be moving up and along the curve to the right as they aggressively optimize their skills portfolio and their value in a PB environment. On the other hand, baby boomers who are nearing retirement probably are not aggressively developing new skills and therefore are more accepting of the boundaries of an AB organization; consequently they are moving down the curve and to the left.

Technically, for those who care, you can't go above the Efficient Skills Frontier because, well, it no longer would be efficient (that is, you absolutely hate what you do).

In a nutshell, that's your challenge. How do you optimize your portfolio of skills so you achieve the greatest return given the risks you are willing to take with respect to lifestyle, love of career, and the investment of resources to identify A.R.T and develop K.I.T.E. ? There is a sweet spot where your wage rate per hour provides you the maximum return given your talent, your skills and the lifestyle you want. I hope you find it.

LEARNING TO SAVE

HOW
TO DEVELOP
THE MINDSET OF
A SAVER

My generations, and others before me, grew up with family owned saving jars that were referred to as Piggy Banks. Basically the concept was that individuals should think like a bank, so if you want to take any money out of the jar, then you must be willing to put something into it. I always thought the concept of Pig and Bank worked well together; however, not in a way that I would use it as a metaphor to teach you about life. Feed the Pig, a catch phrase used among many accountants, seems more like the launch phrase for obesity. Instead, I want you to think of a squirrel. If you watch a squirrel jump from limb to limb and frolic among the trees there is a certain agility a squirrel has mastered, using a relatively large bushy tail for balance. Plus, you have to like the way they save their primary food source so they have nuts to consume during the cold winter months.

So, I have a new mascot that I want you to visualize as you count down your birthdays to age 40. C.H.R.I.S. the agile squirrel. C.H.R.I.S. is my newest acronym to remind you that during the next 10 years you should focus on your Career, value your Health, build your Relationships, and you can only Invest for tomorrow if you learn how to Save for today. Like C.H.R.I.S. you need to store away some of the acorns of your success so you can survive the blustery and volatile winters when pigs get slaughtered. So, with C.H.R.I.S. the agile squirrel fresh in our mind let's discuss savings and the other Algorithms of Value.

THE SIMPLE MATHEMATICS OF SAVINGS

Accounting, my first technical core competence, is the fundamental language of business and personal finance.

I know most people would find this bizarre, but there is a certain elegance about accounting. This elegance manifests itself in a very simple mathematical equation:

$$Savings = Assets - Debts$$

Many people refer to Savings as Wealth, Profits, Net Worth, Net Equity, Shareholders' Equity, and Net Assets. The terms are essentially interchangeable and boils down to what is yours, free and clear of any interests by other parties. Debts include the actual amount you owe someone (e.g. a home mortgage, student loans, credit card obligations, car loans, etc.).

Assets include the tangible stuff you own (e.g. a house, land, cash, investments, etc.) that have a reasonable chance of maintaining some value in the future. Assets could also include intangible assets you possess (e.g. your intelligence, education, relationships, skills, etc.). However, if these assets actually have economic value then they will manifest themselves in future earnings. In other words, intangible assets have value only if you can convert such assets into cash sometime in the future. **During your 30s your principal source of Assets are the monies you will earn from your career.**

However, I will simplify all of the confusing terms and refer to S as Savings, Assets as A and Debts as D. Therefore,

$$S = A - D$$

Like any mathematical equation, the left side must equal the right side, that is, the equation must balance. Try as you might, you cannot destroy this symmetry anymore than refuting other mathematical theorems such as $E = MC^2$.

From this relatively simple equation, there are three irrefutable truths.

1. If you have no Debt, then S = A.
2. Increasing Debt NEVER increases Savings.
3. Savings can never be negative.

Let's take a moment and look at each of these truths individually. The first truth is simple. If you have no debts, then you own 100% of your assets.

The second truth surprises many people since they have been persuaded to believe that only with debt (which is ALWAYS someone else's money) can you create wealth. However, borrowing money does either one of two things: (a) it has no impact on your savings (you borrow $100,000 to buy an asset, like a house) or (b) it decreases your savings (you use your credit card to consume almost anything that will have minimal value in the future; food, clothes, entertainment, electronics, furniture, etc.). **If you borrow money for college, it is not the D that creates wealth, it's what you do with the A (the intangible asset of learning and education)**. If you borrow money to make an investment ("weatherize" your home) it is not the D that increases savings, it's whether the A has a reasonable payback period and return.

The third truth is that S can never be a negative number (just like the E in Einstein's equation). If the left side of your equation is negative, then it means you are mathematically insolvent (i.e. you are on a path to bankruptcy). Technically, negative Savings is Debt. In other words, D > A, because there is no S, there is no symmetry, there is no balance.

If you consume more than you produce, then you fall into irrefutable truth number three. You are broke! Unfortunately for these poor souls, rising debt payments will continue to divert money away from the possibility of pursuing any productive endeavors. Many people who are broke will spend their life as an indentured serf to someone (usually the government or some other quasi-government entity, like a bank). However, for those people who have an opportunity to produce more than they will consume, then it may be possible to dig out of this hole of despair. However, this is very difficult once you start down a path of funding your deficits with Debt.

Many educated individuals in the United States who are in their late twenties unfortunately fall into category three. That is, they are broke. They borrowed extensively in the hope their education could be converted into an income stream that would be sufficient to live a reasonable lifestyle and pay their debt. They were wrong. At the end of 2014, the average student loan debt was approaching $30,000; increasing in four decades from virtually zero to an aggregate amount of more than a trillion dollars. Most of this debt is owed to the U.S. Federal Government. For many individuals, future wages will not be sufficient to live a reasonable lifestyle and repay these obligations. Consequently, current repayment plans will essentially garnish up to 15% of an individual's wages, essentially into perpetuity.

THE WARPED MATHEMATICS OF DEBT

Most financial advisors, and the companies they represent, want you to focus on maximizing A and consequently all of their discussions regarding S (which often in this context is referred to as Wealth) relates to how you grow A. In fact, from their perspective, the more money you borrow the better. Why? Because the fees they generate for themselves are based on A. The larger the A and the more you change the composition of A (trading stocks and bonds), the more money your "advisors" make.

Creditors want you to maximize D. Why? Because the more D you have and the longer you take to repay D, the more interest you pay to them. However, creditors will never directly discuss D; instead they will focus on a monthly payment to repay D. Sometimes the lower the payment the better because it will take you longer to pay off D. Their objective is to get you to the point where your monthly payment is not enough to pay for interest, penalties and fees. Once they achieve this objective, your D (which is your creditor's A) will continue to grow into perpetuity (the true beauty of compound interest if you're a creditor). This is why "deferment" of student loan obligations are so insidious to you (and your peers) and so attractive to the U.S. Federal government (or other private creditors).

All lenders are predators. No one loans you money because they believe debt is in your best interest. Just because you can borrow money doesn't mean you should.

Most financial institutions are in the dual profession of convincing you they can maximize A while at the same time doing everything they can to help you increase D. To them they have no conflict, since it is not their goal to help you increase or maximize S. Truth is, this is way beyond their core competence anyway (that is, they are probably not the people who should be advising you on your professional careers). Oh, by the way, there is positive arbitrage (when the amount of interest earned is more than the interest paid), but only for the financial institutions. If the banks have positive arbitrage, then you have negative arbitrage. This is why, my sons, that most people who love D have no S.

My advice is exactly opposite of most financial advisors and creditors. I want you to increase S by reducing D (economists call this "deleveraging"). In fact, only when D is zero would I even begin a discussion regarding the best way to invest A. Otherwise I will tell you just to use A to pay off D. If they could, bankers would probably charge me with blasphemy for making such a statement! In fact, despite what others might tell you, I can almost guarantee you that if you focus on investing A while you still have D, then your S will slowly fade away.

As a result, if you don't want to become an indentured servant to a creditor, then there are some very simple rules you must follow with respect to D.

Rule #1: The only reasonable use of D is to buy a home, which I will discuss in the next chapter.

Rule #2: Never use D to fund a new business opportunity, especially if you personally guarantee the debt. If you have a good business idea, then sell some of your equity in the venture.

Rule #3: Never use D to smooth your future consumption patterns. It is a reckless strategy during a time when you are building your career and your career options.

Rule #4: If you use D to pay for anything that has to do with current or future employment (education and transportation), then you must have a rational expectation that there is a reasonable return on such an investment. For example, it makes no sense to incur $100,000 of student loans in order to secure a minimum wage job or to pay a $400 monthly car payment for a part-time job that pays $400 a month. In a moment I will explore this in some additional detail.

Rule #5: If you use D for any purpose, you must minimize D and strive to pay back D as soon as possible. In almost all cases, you created D because you consumed more than you produced. The only way D can be repaid is if you now produce more than you consume!

You must always remember that when S is your source for consumption you are tapping into your reserves. If you are tapping into your reserves, then your cost of living is exceeding your monthly paycheck. On the other hand, if you use D to finance your consumption, you are creating a future obligation that will increase your monthly spending and reduce your future savings. Because this obligation is principally fixed (until the debt is repaid), you are also becoming more fragile financially because you will have less flexibility to adjust your future spending should the need arise.

It is critical, before age 40, that S is approaching two years of your projected annual spending. That is, if you plan to spend $100,000 in the year after you turn 40, then S = $200,000. If you own your home, then S can be split between relatively liquid cash investments and the relatively illiquid equity invested in your home. If you don't own your home, then S should equal your liquid investments. If so, then, and only then, should you begin to focus on how to invest A to maximize your earnings (which I will explore in more detail in the next chapter, Investing With Wisdom).

As you can now understand, if you learn to avoid debt, then the above equation boils down to a very simple theorem. That is,

$$S = A$$

You will never have real wealth unless you learn to optimize S. The question now becomes, how do you generate

GETTING TO 40

savings? Well, let's think of an asset in a very traditional way. An asset is cash and cash is money. How do you get money. Well, there are only four ways you get money. You steal it, you borrow it, someone gives it to you, or you earn it. Between now and age 40, **the only way you should get money is to earn it.** As you now understand, the way you earn money is to focus on your career and create your future. If you are in a PB career, what you earn should reflect the value of what you produce. If you follow the guidelines in this book I truly believe you will achieve optimal earnings. However, you will not generate S unless you consume less than you produce.

Moreover, if you ever hope to launch your own business venture someday, you must learn how to manage your personal financial affairs. There are synergies in both endeavors. The simple equations you are learning are fundamental to any viable economic activity.

THE MATHEMATICS OF CONSUMPTION

Once again, I will simplify all of the confusing terms in personal finance and refer to spending or consumption as C and wages/production/income as earnings, or E. Therefore, to become a saver, you must achieve the following outcome:

$$C < E$$

How much you will save during your 30s will depend on how great the difference is between what you consume (spend) and the wages you earn (what your produce).

C < E is the fundamental tenet to what I call the Agile Advantage. In other words, you must do more than bal-

154

ance your budget with C = E. Basically, it requires you to live below your means and that you absolutely do not borrow against tomorrow's income. **In a bit of a paradox, you must aggressively pursue gratification with respect to your career and delay gratification when it comes to your spending.** The challenge is when to switch on the behaviors that benefit your career while at the same time turning off these same behaviors when it comes to consumption.

To achieve C < E you must be a smart and savvy consumer. I don't mean miserly. I don't mean cheap. I don't mean hoarding. I mean clever. I mean wise. I mean smart, but frugal. For example, you already know C cannot be less than E if you use Debt to fund your consumption (the mantra of buy now and pay later). Unless you learn to minimize C relative to E you will never be a saver. If you are not a saver, you will never achieve the Agile Advantage.

It probably seems obvious but it's important for you to understand why saving is so important. There are two primary reasons you must save during your 30s:

- To Avoid Debt
- To Invest in Career Opportunities

Let me take a couple of minutes and discuss in a bit more detail D, or Debt. If you have no savings, then the only reason you should ever borrow money is to make a wise investment. An investment is wise only if it can generate sufficient cash flows to pay not only the interest on the Debt but also pay back the debt. You can never pay back Debt unless the investment you make will generate future savings. In other words, the debt you borrow must be able to decrease C (e.g. an investment in energy saving gadgets for your home) or increase E (that is, an investment in skills and education). Consequently, not only does C have to be less than E, but now the incremental increase in E or the incremental decrease in C must be sufficient to justify the investment. In other words, it is the incremental change in E and/or C that generates the cash flow necessary to pay off the Debt (and the interest on the Debt).

$$\uparrow \Delta E \; + \; \downarrow \Delta C \; > \; Debt + Interest\ on\ Debt$$

Most people don't realize they must generate future savings (which is synonymous with PROFITS) to pay back money they borrow and the related interest expense. Moreover, poor investment decisions always generate insufficient E and/or not enough reduction in C to pay back D. When this happens, Savings will always decline. If D can not be paid back then bankruptcy is inevitable. Finally, you must remember this universal truth: **Money that is borrowed to fund consumption will ALWAYS increase C and NEVER increase E!**

Saving is the most important resource to fund consumption when your production declines in the future. For most people, a permanent decline in production usually occurs when they retire. However, when you retire, or if you retire, will be a function of your savings relative to your projected future spending until you die. During your 30s this should not be a primary concern. However, you should be mindful that the day will come when your savings will be the primary predictor of your future lifestyle. A lack of savings will limit your ability to spend in the future. That is, you will be more fragile.

You should also understand that if you judiciously accumulate assets today, these assets have the potential to provide you a return in the future. That is, not only will you earn money based on your skills, but you also will earn money on the capital that you provide to others. In other words, you become a source of investment that helps to sustain not only your lifestyle; but hopefully improves the lifestyle of others that reside in your community. Ironically, your savings can also be used to exploit those individuals who borrow to fund a lifestyle that they can't afford.

THE VALUE OF YOUR TIME

Your time has value. How you value your time is one of the most important variables in any economic decision model. As individuals our goal is to allocate our time in a manner that optimizes health, happiness and success. Truth is, most of us don't. The reason we don't optimize our time is because most of us have no idea where we spend our time and the relative value of our time.

Each day we spend our time in three basic areas:

- Career
- Leisure
- Sleep

Time is precious because it's scarce and perishable. We cannot relive those moments that are in our past. The last ten seconds I spent writing the previous sentence are now gone forever. I can't recapture it. **Because you cannot "save" time it is important that you don't waste time.** All of us can identify examples of time we waste in our careers, time we lose doing things we don't enjoy and time we lie in bed awake when we should be sleeping. You need to minimize the time you waste. The best way to minimize the time you waste is to put a value on your time.

For lack of a better metric, the value of your time should be benchmarked off what you earn. The value you receive to trade an hour of your skills should be no less than the value you place on an hour of your leisure time. Therefore, if you invest 2,000 hours a year in your career and earn $50,000, then the value of your time in today's environment begins at $25 an hour (you should make your own calculation; but I will use $25 an hour as the value of time in the examples below). A minute of your time is worth approximately 42 cents (Uber, by the way, pays it drivers 15 cents a minute, or $9 per hour). In any event, now you can assess the trade-offs related to competing alternatives.

To make things a bit easier, I'm going to designate sleep time as a cushion, or a reserve, that you can tap if you need to work more (career) or if you want more free time (leisure) during your typical day. In other words, only because of your relative youth, if you need to work more hours, or hang out with your friends, you can choose to sleep less, without penalty (or reward) with respect to the value of your time. However, that said, you need to remember a good night sleep is still important if you are going to sustain a certain level of health and productivity. Therefore, at some point, sleep becomes too valuable to trade.

Doing things you like will always have more value than doing things you hate. I love racquetball. I hate yard work. Consequently, I value an hour invested in each activity totally differently. I might love racquetball so much that I would pay $25 an hour just to enjoy the game. On the other hand, I might hate yard work so much that someone would have to pay me $50 an hour to do it. Therefore, it is an easy decision to pay a landscaper $25 for one hour worth of work so I can enjoy playing racquetball for an hour.

One reason you want to increase the value of your output (as discussed in detail in Creating Your Future) is so you have the resources to pay others to do the things you hate and you can spend more time doing the things you love. Individuals who place a low value on their time (or have others who believe their time has little value) will usually spend a higher percentage of their day doing things they don't really like. No woman should bear 100% of the responsibility for child rearing. However, single mothers who have minimal skills have little choice but to accept this responsibility (even if it is something they don't enjoy) because the value of their output is not high enough to pay others to take care of their children.

One of the best ways for everyone to spend more time doing the things they love is to minimize the time they waste. The best way to minimize the time you waste is to put a price tag on your cost of misery and then change your behavior. I used to love watching the Cleveland Browns. It's how I would enjoy a Sunday afternoon during the Fall. It required six hours of my free time (4.5 hours for the game; 1.5 hours for the commute). The value of my output is much greater than $25 an hour. However, even using this benchmark, watching the wretched Browns was clearing not worth the cost of my time ($150), which you could double once you added in the cost of the ticket and the afternoon munchies. When it became clear I could tape the game, start to watch it an hour before completion, fast forward through all of the dismal commercials and invest an hour in the entire event, even this one hour seemed hardly worth it, and that was when they won.

All of us are constantly reallocating our time among the basic categories of Career, Leisure and Sleep and between things we love to do and things we hate to do. Even time we may consider as priceless (e.g. time we spend with our kids) is still subject to a daily decision model that requires us to allocate our time among competing priorities. Calculate the value of your time, track how you spend it, understand the cost of competing activities and reallocate your time to those things that bring you greater joy and more value. Learn to fill the gaps of dead time with more productive activities.

PATTERNS OF CONSUMPTION

It is unlikely you will ever become a saver unless you understand what you consume, why you consume and the real cost of your consumption. Let's begin with a discussion about transportation which, after shelter and food, is the most expensive item in most family's daily budgets. For purposes of this discussion you're a transportation junkie (I will refer to you as TJ). Even though you crave driving you still recognize that you need to learn to save and therefore your goal is to minimize your cost of C. What process should you go through (which will be the identical process for every item you consume — especially those that cost you money or cost you time) to minimize C?

Step #1 Start With Zero

If you goal is to minimize consumption, then you start with zero. You don't start with a percentage of your income. You don't start with a government recommended amount. You don't start with what your friend thinks. You start with zero in your budget. You start with zero because your goal is to minimize consumption.

Starting with zero makes you think about why you spend what you spend. There are basically two reasons you spend money. You spend money on things you need and things you want. For example, you may need transportation to go to work; you may want transportation to visit friends.

Step #2 Define The Metric That Measures Usage

You should identify a basic unit of measure for everything that you consume. For example, with respect to transportation the most common fundamental unit of measure is a mile. Without a basic unit of measure you cannot compare competing scenarios. The way to compare competing scenarios is to complete the following sentence, "What is my cost per _____?"

Step #3 Determine Consumption Levels

Pick a time horizon (day, month or year) and make an educated guess regarding your level of consumption or usage. How many miles do you drive in a year? What is the breakdown of miles between needs (e.g. transportation to work) and wants (e.g. visit to friends and family). For most individuals, going to and from work is the biggest need for their own personal transportation. Therefore, for purposes of this discussion, I am going to make a very simple assumption. TJ drives 9,000 miles a year to and from work (36 miles roundtrip for each of the 250 days that he works). He drives another 3,000 miles a year to visit friends and families. His total consumption; 12,000 miles a year.

Step #4 Calculate Your Cost of Consumption

For any individual consumption item (a lower case "c") your total costs of consumption is:

$$c = usage \times cost\ per\ usage$$

If you know c you can calculate your cost per usage and if you know your cost per usage you can solve for c.

In TJ's case, because he is "learning to save" he is **doing the math before he makes a commitment** (hint: the larger the commitment the more important it is that you do the math before you spend). Therefore, he wants to figure out c under various scenarios.

Like most Americans TJ values his freedom and he wants the real American dream, a nice automobile. What is TJ's cost of independence. TJ doesn't want to calculate this cost himself so he Googles "cost of car ownership" and discovers that the Internal Revenue Service ("IRS") believes (in 2015) the average cost of personal transportation is **57.5 cents per mile.** That's good enough for TJ and therefore he determines the **12,000 miles** he drives a year will cost him **$6,900** (75% of this amount, or $5,175 is work related; 25% or $1,725 is his cost to visit friends and family).

A quick aside. Every cost per usage is derived from some financial model. Like any model, the more you understand the variables with respect to the model, the better your understanding of the risks that the model could be wrong. In this case, the IRS has four basic variables with respect to it's model (the cost of a car, the car's useful life, the cost of gasoline and the cost of insurance). For example, if TJ paid $22,500 for his car, drove it 60,000 miles over five years, paid $3 for a gallon of gas that drove him 20 miles and $600 a year for insurance, then he would hit the IRS benchmark. TJ figures the vehicle cost is 37.5 cents a mile and his costs to operate is 20 cents a mile. However, if any of these figures are wrong (his car costs more, gasoline is more expensive, or if he drives more miles during the year), then the model is wrong (GIGO). Moreover, like most costs, the above model does not include indirect costs of transportation (environmental costs, infrastructure needs, etc.).

Step #5 Understand Your Cost of Consumption

TJ values his freedom. However, in his quest for independence he is becoming a bit concerned that he is losing some of his flexibility. He is becoming more fragile. He recognizes that once he buys his car he has incurred a significant fixed cost. In addition, the entire reason he owns his car is to drive it, so essentially he has converted a variable cost into a fixed cost. TJ doesn't want a $575 fixed cost every month and so he wonders, is there a better alternative. Plus, it begins to bother him that every trip he takes costs 57.5 cents per mile. The 20 mile trip to visit his friend, $11.50. The 260 mile round trip to see his parents, $150. It's depressing. TJ thinks Uber and decides to make his entire cost structure variable. However, at a cost in excess of $1 per mile this doesn't make any sense. Public transit is more reasonable at $100 per month but TJ loses some of his freedom and flexibility. TJ's environment has relatively nice weather and reasonable infrastructure for biking, but TJ values his time and believes it will take an extra two hours a day just to ride his bike to and from work. Plus, TJ doesn't particularly like biking. TJ values his time at $25 an hour (equivalent to what he earns in his job) and therefore the opportunity cost of biking to work of $12,500 (500 hours a year at $25 an hour) seems too expensive.

Step #6 Compare Costs of Consumption To Wages

TJ earns $50,000 in gross wages. After federal, state, local and mandated payroll taxes (FICA), TJ's net cash flow for the coming year is $37,500 (75% of his gross wages). If TJ buys the car he wants, his $6,900 annual transportation expenses will eat up 18.4% of his cash flows.

Step #7 Make a Decision and Build a Strategy

TJ decides to buy his car but he is not happy that his transportation costs will consume approximately 20% of his wages and there is little he can do during the next five years (the length of his car loan) to control this fixed cost. However, he now recognizes that the only way he can reduce his consumption in the future is to:

↓*Usage or* ↓*Cost Per Usage*

TJ can decrease his usage by driving less. The best way for TJ to drive less is to be more efficient in his consumption patterns (ride sharing, occasional use of public transit, perhaps ride his bike once in awhile). In other words, a reduction in usage will help reduce TJ's variable costs (principally gasoline costs).

TJ can decrease his cost per usage by getting more miles out of his existing vehicle. In other words, he takes excellent care of his vehicle and drives it for more years and for more miles. For example, if he drives his vehicle for 12 years and 120,000 miles, then he has driven down his average fixed costs to 18.75 cents a mile (a 50% reduction from his original projection). After five years, once his car is paid for, he would have no fixed costs in years 6 to 10. **TJ is now less fragile financially because he has eliminated his fixed costs and all of his transportation costs are now variable.** Even with no increase in wages, his transportation budget is now only 6.4% of his annual cash flows, or $2,400 (12,000 miles x 20 cents a mile) a year. Of course, TJ could have driven down his cost per usage at time of purchase if he would have substituted a vehicle that achieved 40 miles to a gallon of gas versus 20 miles. In fact, he would have reduced his annual fuel costs from $1,800 a year (or 15 cents a mile) to $900 a year (or 7.5 cents a mile).

Step #8 Understand What Drives Human Behavior

Owning your own automobile is a very big part of human culture, especially in the United States. For many, it IS the American Dream. The automotive industry spends a significant amount on advertising to help you behave in a certain way. This behavior pulls you and pushes you to buy (or lease) the perfect car that conveys a certain image or fits a certain lifestyle. In addition, the objective of the car industry is to maximize the number of cars you buy in your lifetime. What maximizes value for the producer minimizes value for the consumer. In other words, the more inefficient your consumption the happier you make the industry. Churn is their mantra.

You will never learn to save unless you understand that how you behave as a buyer is exactly the opposite of how a seller wants you to behave. For example, when you recognize the purpose of transportation is to physically move you from Point A to Point B in the quickest, safest and most cost effective way possible, then you have achieved the mindset of a wise consumer.

Step #9 Develop A Model To Measure Efficiency

Most of you will avoid this step because the mathematics are a bit complex. I don't blame you. However, it's important that you understand the concept and therefore I will walk you through the process.

I measure efficiency on a scale of 0 to 1. As the scale approaches zero you are very efficient and as it approaches 1 you are very inefficient. There are two primary variables when it comes to transportation. The value of your time and the cost of transportation, relative to your wages.

You can calculate a transportation efficiency percentage (TEP) using the following formula:

$$TEP = \frac{(Opportunity\ Cost\ of\ Capital\ +\ Commuting\ Costs)}{Daily\ Wages}$$

where

Opportunity Cost of Capital =
Commuting Time x Wage Rate Per Hour

For example, if you earn $11.50 per hour (for an 8 hour work day) and it takes 30 minutes to drive 10 miles to work (at a cost of 57.5 cents a mile), then you have a TEP of .25. If your commuting time to work is 1 hour and you drive 20 miles, then your TEP = .50. If you drive more than 6 hours to and from work, then your TEP =1. Candidly, when TEP exceeds 1 it doesn't make sense to work. In fact, it probably doesn't make sense to work if your TEP > .5.

You can reduce a high TEP if you convert commuting time to productive time. For example, listening to podcasts for skills development or riding a bike for exercise. Or, you might drive TEP to zero by working at home. In any event, the conclusions should be intuitive. The more time you waste commuting and the higher the actual cost of your travel relative to your wages, the less efficient your transportation.

Lower wage workers who own their own cars and commute to work will always be the most inefficient consumers of transportation. Although they may value their opportunity cost of capital as low, they tend to have very high transportation costs relative to their incomes. The only way for them to become more efficient (i.e. with their current job) is to use their commuting time to improve their skills and/or to take advantage of lower-cost public transit. They could also find a job closer to home or move somewhere closer to their employer (of course, these decisions also involve economic and other lifestyle trade-offs).

The point of all of this is to begin to recognize the profile of the most agile individuals. On one hand, people who don't own a car keep all of their transportation costs variable. In other words, they pay for transportation only when they need it. If they use mass transit, then there is a greater likelihood their commuting time is productive. If, they ride a bike or walk, then their commuting time is replaced with healthy exercise.

On the other hand, individuals who are in perpetual debt for their transportation needs are the least agile. Many are inefficient in their transportation patterns. They don't car pool or ride share. Their cars depreciate quicker because of excessive miles or poor maintenance. Some buy more expensive and less fuel efficient vehicles because it helps build their "image." They may have more accidents because of distractions during their boring commutes and incur higher insurance costs. Because their financing terms are usually for periods equal to or greater than 60 months they get bored and roll over their negative equity into a new car with higher and higher monthly car payments. They don't understand concepts like TEP. They have no idea what it really costs them to drive. Yet, transportation costs continue to make up a larger and larger percentage of their total fixed costs.

Transportation costs are like all costs. What you don't spend you save. You need to think about why you drive what you drive. You need to think about when you drive and where you drive. You need to have the right data so you can make better decisions.

WHERE DOES ALL THE WASTE COME FROM?

Until you have to move out of a home that you have lived in for several years it is difficult to appreciate how much stuff you buy. In preparation for listing my parents' home for sale I spent the past six months purging years of clutter. Trash bag after trash bag was hauled to the curb, multiple car loads of donations were delivered to Goodwill Industries and a lot of stuff was given away. I would not say my parents were hoarders, but similar to most of us it is difficult to throw things away that you purchased over the years or things that were given to you by others (gifts, family heirlooms and other stuff that we inherit). Perhaps it is our way of believing that if we don't throw it out then it wasn't a wasteful expenditure on our part (or someone else's).

Where did the "waste" come from? Well, technology obsolescence contributed a significant amount as I tossed out telephones, cell phones, computers, printers, 8 track tapes, VHS tapes, CDs, floppy disks, tape recorders, typewriters, cameras, TVs, cables and related items. Holiday related items

You can't learn to save until you understand why you waste.

were probably next; lights that no longer work, old plastic Xmas trees and ornaments, gifts that were never opened or never used, festive plates and glassware. Lots of clothes, shoes, and outerwear made the trip to the donation center. Certainly poor organization and inventory management contributed to the waste as multiple tools, household cleaning supplies and similar items were tossed or given away.

Unfortunately many of the things my parents probably expected to hand down to other family members went unclaimed. Of course, this is not surprising. All of us have our own stuff which is reinforced every time I walk through my garage, basement and other rooms throughout our house. **Our homes have become nothing more than storage facilities for all the stuff we buy.** Until you personally go through such a process it's difficult to appreciate how much our excess and inefficient consumption drains our savings and poisons our environment.

WHAT TYPE OF CONSUMER ARE YOU?

Most people have no idea what they consume, how much they consume and their real cost of consumption. Their spending patterns are based entirely on what they make, what they borrow and what others subsidize on their behalf.

You cannot learn to save unless you understand where you spend, how you spend and why you spend. In other words, you need to understand your pattern of consumption. The best way to understand your pattern of consumption is to either summarize where you spent your money in the last three months, or at a minimum, where you spent your money in the last 30 days. Then you need to ask yourself what type of consumer are you and what type of consumer do you want to be? Do you want to be Wise and thrifty (W.T.) or Wasteful, Thankless and Foolish (W.T.F.).

I'm ashamed to admit it, but historically I've been a W.T.F. consumer. W.T.F. consumers tend to:

- Seek status by owning the newest and best
- Plunder resources for ease and convenience
- Acquire nice things they use sparingly
- Buy things "on sale" that they don't need and won't use
- Act on impulse

W.T.F. consumers waste resources. People waste resources for a lot of different reasons. Sometimes it's because they are lazy and it's too inconvenient to "turn off the lights" or separate the garbage into recyclables. Most of the time it is because they don't feel accountable or responsible for their actions. They keep the lights on and the thermostat high in winter (and low in summer). People in poverty waste resources because they receive many products and services for free, or at a heavily subsidized price. On the other hand, wealthy people waste resources because of their propensity towards abundance. In both cases, a sense of entitlement can easily engulf both groups where cost doesn't matter because someone else is paying for our irresponsible and often reckless behavior.

Some W.T.F. consumers actually have a spending addiction. Spending helps them assuage pain or increase pleasure. Like any habit, repeated behavior becomes harder to stop over time. Many of them actually need professional counseling.

Sometimes people lack awareness of their consumption habits and the education to make better decisions. Often people waste resources because the costs are borne by other individuals and their communities. Many producers, distributors and retailers actually encourage inefficient consumption patterns; especially those entities that sell based on price versus those who sell based on value. However, even monopolies (e.g. public utilities with large fixed costs) require a certain level of consumption to rationalize their business models. The U.S. Post Office might be one of the largest facilitators of waste in the world. I guess this is why we call most of the stuff in our mailbox junk mail.

For me, the good news is that I am now more aware how W.T. consumers behave and I am making the transition. Wise and Thrifty consumers:

- Understand consumption models like cost per use
- Work to extend the useful life of a product
- Favor products that are longer lasting
- Use resources only when they are needed
- Embrace renewable energy systems
- Invest in technology that helps them consume less
- Seek data and information on patterns of consumption
- Focus on usage efficiency
- Recycle bottles, newspapers, etc.
- Donate items that still have value to others

As you probably guessed, W.T. consumers tend to be concerned about the environmental footprint of the items they buy. It bothers them when they read about tragic accidents in foreign sweatshops. It troubles them that animals are tortured just so we can consume them at a low price. It concerns them when other countries pollute their environment just so we can buy products that often we don't need, or want. Many are not environmentalists and vegetarians and yet consumption patterns and supply chains matter to them. When they waste anything it feels like they are burning money and adding to a pending ecological disaster. Their mantra of "reuse, reduce, recycle" is part of the daily lexicon they use to describe how they live.

So they have discipline and feedback loops that track what they spend, how they consume and why they waste.

W.T. consumers don't save because they want more money. They save to make our world a better place to live. They save because they want a brighter future.

W.T. consumers think about how to unlock the efficiency of consumption. They understand that when they waste resources, they actually decrease their personal savings rate because of inefficient spending patterns. They are cost aware. They think about how to minimize cost per use (e.g. the running shoe that last 50 miles). They recognize that sometimes the more expensive item that lasts longer is actually a better value (e.g. if you amortize a quality bike over the miles ridden it actually can become pretty cheap). Moreover, they are able to capture this value because they can tap into their savings to make opportunistic purchases. **W.T. consumers understand that the power and flexibility to walk away from a "deal" is the only way to obtain the best price.**

Often times I wish there was an app that would provide usage data for all purchases and calculate a cost per use (e.g. how many miles will I get out of a quality running shoe versus a cheap ... and often counterfeit alternative). A type of robo adviser that would nudge me into better purchasing decisions.

W.T. consumers understand the concept of Arbitrage Squeeze which is why they can reject products (and services) that are new, shiny and the latest and greatest. Arbitrage Squeeze simply means that over time, especially in a competitive marketplace, technology and various best practices will narrow the performance and functionality between the best and worst; whether it's the variance in the performance of sports professionals or the functionality of the latest mobile phone. In such an environment, patience can be a virtue. W.T. consumers know that often the best financial choice is not to drive the new car off the lot or unwrap the newest and slickest iPhone. They recognize that often its better to repair than replace.

The good news is that you are coming of age when "smart data" will give you much better information with respect to consumption patterns and the related costs. For example, several benefits of a smart utility grid is the ability to provide real time feedback of energy use and flexible real time pricing to nudge behavior to desired outcomes; allowing you to minimize use during periods of peak demand and insight on how to reduce overall consumption.

The bad news is that it's very difficult to be a W.T. consumer when the U.S. economy continuously programs you to be a W.T.F. consumer. Basically, you are encouraged (stealthy) not to save. In fact, most stimuli you experience not only nudges you to spend, but encourages you to borrow to fund your consumption. Nothing wets the appetite more of a W.T.F. consumer than a jazzy credit card that rewards consumption with "points" (to fuel more consumption) and provides extended payment plans. Their paper mâche lives are created with layers of debt as they acquire the perfect home, expensive cars and other material things that convey status and the need to have it all now. Like so many others, the life of easy pleasures they seek today will end painfully with the hard choices they will be forced to make tomorrow.

The entire U.S. economy (and perhaps the world economy) would collapse if the consumption driven debt fueled United States switched from a W.T.F. to a W.T. mindset. That is, the significant decrease in demand caused by less spending would increase unemployment and idle capacity to levels not seen since the depression. Here's the paradox though; **what may be good for the U.S. economy is not good for you.**

In closing, it's easy to forget that your consumption patterns will favor more intangible services including purchases of virtual goods (music, apps, books). Regardless, W.T.F. consumers approach such purchases using the same process that would use to acquire a tangible product. Even today I have too many apps on my iPhone that provide minimal utility and therefore have a very high cost per use.

INSURANCE AND THE PROBABILITY OF LOSS

Insurance exists to protect you against a financial loss in the future (e.g., a serious illness, a bad car accident, a fire in your home) in exchange for a cash payment you make today. You can insure almost anything. The important thing to keep in mind is that what you pay reflects the probability of loss. For example, if I want to ensure my $20,000 car against the risk of theft and the chance of theft in Cleveland is 1 out of 200 (.5%), then a fair premium (before the insurance company's overhead) to ensure against theft is $100. In an efficient and competitive market, there is a reasonably good chance that what you pay to insure against a possible loss will be fair. However, when there is no competitive market (e.g. product warranties that you purchase at time of sale) you can almost guarantee what you pay significantly exceeds your risk of loss. Therefore, savers usually never make this type of purchase. The only time when you probably should buy insurance in an uncompetitive market is when an uninsured loss could wreck havoc on your finances (which is why most people need health insurance).

Expected Premium = Amount of Loss x Probability of Loss

The greater your savings the easier it is to self insure for many risks. In a way, the premiums you don't pay to a third party actually become a primary source of your savings. I don't need disability or life insurance because I have sufficient resources to cover these risks myself. Always try to make sure you have a very clear understanding what specific risk you are trying to insure. Insure those risks that have a low probability of a catastrophic outcome but would represent a significant cost (e.g., professional and personal liability).

Insurance is always a zero sum bet. What you gain the other party loses. It is also asymmetric. If your number comes up (e.g., someone steals your car) your payoff will be many multiples times your original payment. In return for the certainty of your downside (the premium you paid) you receive the uncertainty of the upside. Of course, there is no point in buying insurance from a party that might go out of business, especially at the time the insurance becomes the most valuable. Therefore the longer the expected time before payout (e.g., life insurance) the more important it is for the insurer to have an impeccable reputation.

LOWER YOUR BREAKEVEN COST OF LIVING

I want you to put aside any budgets you've been using and do two things. First, for the last three months build an analysis of where you actually spent your money. You can summarize this budget anyway you want, but the more detail the better. If you don't have the detail, then for the next three months start to keep track of where you spend you money. As you know, there are now various apps that will help you capture this information; but sometimes writing things down yourself will somehow have a bit more power of analysis.

Once you have this information, calculate some key metrics for yourself. For example, what was your cost per meal (including both food and drink)? Look at your utility bills? What are the fixed and variable costs of your bills? For the variable costs, what was the cost per usage? For example, for your water bill, what was the cost per flush or per shower? For your electric bill how many kilowatt hours of power did you consume? Why? How often do you keep the lights burning, or the temperature high (in winter) or low (in summer). How often did you shop for clothing? What did you buy? Why? How does it compare to your current inventory? Just how many shirts, pair of jeans, shoes, etc. do you need?

After you accumulate this data, then ask yourself the following: How much do I really have to spend to live just above the poverty line. Forget for a moment any fixed transportation costs or housing expense (house or rental payment). How much do you need to spend to barely get by. Then ask yourself, what do I need to spend to have a reasonable standard of living. Finally, once you complete this process, compare it to what you spent for the 3 months of your analysis. What did you learn?

What you should learn is that you probably can get by spending a lot less than you do. I'm not asking you to reduce your spending to your bare bones breakeven point. I'm just asking you to have much better insight where this point is and what changes in behavior you could make if you ever needed to achieve this threshold. I want you to understand your preferences and why they are important to you.

Now, let's look at your total cost of living ("C") by including monthly fixed expenses for housing, transportation and debt service payments. You will always be more agile (especially during a period in your life when you need the greatest mobility) if your fixed costs ("F") represent a smaller percentage of your total spending relative to your variable expenses ("V").

$$C = F + V$$

Therefore, as V/C approaches 1 you will be the most flexible when it comes to your ability to make lifestyle changes that will benefit your career. It would provide you the flexibility to weather crises that will make others vulnerable. Conversely, when F/C approaches 1 you are the most fragile and even minor shocks in your life will have tremendously adverse outcomes.

The better you understand what you consume the more you will have greater insight into how changes in prices impact your lifestyle. Your personal inflation (or deflation) rate should never approximate changes in the consumer price index because you don't consume the same basket of goods that is used in this calculation. In other words, how price changes impact you in the future will be unique to you based on how you spend.

MINIMIZE UNFUNDED FUTURE OBLIGATIONS

You need to begin to understand the concept of unfunded future obligations, especially if there is a reasonable likelihood that you will personally pay this liability. An unfunded future obligation is a cost that you incur today that you don't have to pay until tomorrow and therefore you don't set aside the money today.

Next to retirement, children are probably your greatest unfunded financial obligation, especially when it comes to post high school education. In 2014, the average cost of a four-year public and a four-year private on campus college education was approximately $92,000 and $180,000 respectively. These costs include tuition, fees, room, board, books, supplies, transportation and other expenses. **The way to pay for this obligation in the future is to save the necessary funds today.** Specifically, if you have a child born in 2017 you should plan to have no less than $100,000 set aside in 2035 to pay for that child's college education. In other words, if you plan for your children to go to college you should start to save no less than $5,000 a year to meet this commitment and obligation.

Most parents significantly underestimate the cost of college, principally because of the relative ease of securing federal loans to pay for a student's post high school education. Perhaps ironically, with respect to federal financial aid guidelines, the more you save, the more you pay. The good news is there are a number of trends which should reduce the cost of your children's education in the future. First, the entire financial model is changing, rapidly. You should expect to see an explosion of post high school education choices, with much easier access through online training and interaction.

Second, you should expect to see a greater push to link the cost of post high school education to the earnings that such education should generate. For example, graduates would be required to pay 3% of their earnings for the next 20 years. Therefore, if average projected annual wages were $50,000, then a college degree should cost $30,000. In other words, educators will have greater accountability for the quality and value of their degrees relative to economic output. Diplomas and certificates that cannot demonstrate that they produce some type of tangible value for their recipients will begin to lose their luster in the future.

Third, the U.S. federal and state governments are moving closer and closer to making the cost of post high school public education a federal entitlement to its citizens (basically shifting the cost of college education to all taxpayers). Whether making two-year colleges free or through hyper aggressive forgiveness of federal student loans, you should expect these trends to continue.

Over the next ten years you must anticipate a lot of unknown contingencies. The cost of your children's education is only one of many. However, I'm confident you can minimize this risk if you raise your kids to be responsible adults. If so, then together, you will have a great opportunity to minimize the debt that is anchoring so many families to an uncertain future. Scholarships will always be available, kids can work, room and board is still "free" while living at home, transportation needs are minimal when your kids should be sitting in a classroom and a litany of other ideas can greatly minimize the cost of tomorrow's education. In any event, in today's environment you should plan to support your children's cost of living through a post high school education process; probably until your kids are 21 or 22.

SEEKING HIGH QUALITY USED (OR UNDERUTILIZED) GOODS FOR FREE

My parents', and my baby boom generation, are beginning one of the largest liquidation events in history. Through death and downsizing we are moving out of homes into smaller and less complex environments. As discussed earlier, these homes contain the legacy of the greatest consumption binge in modern history. Furniture, housewares, appliances, pool tables, hot tubs, pianos, tools, entertainment centers, and numerous other items, many high quality prized family possessions, are now essentially junk headed to the trash heap. Many families, and I know we will be one of them, will be happy just to give the stuff away.

I know cheaper imports, stock on the shelfs of Walmart, Target and Ikea, are favored by your generation. It is one reason that the value of traditional home furnishings have plummeted and no one is even interested in "second hand" merchandise. In addition, a lot of the stuff is actually too big for many of today's smaller homes. However, you might be surprised, that with a little planning and foresight, there is a tremendous number of things you might need (or want) that you could acquire for minimal dollars. Estate sales, antique dealers, Craigslist, consignment stores and other entities are becoming outlets for a significant amount of high quality products.

Look for new apps that soon will match local sellers and buyers and facilitate the exchange of unused and excess inventory that resides in the homes of our generation. Some websites like Yerdle already offer underutilized goods — youth sports equipment, musical instruments, electronics, and other items that tend to gather in neighborhood closets and garages — for free.

MONETIZE INTANGIBLE ASSETS

You probably don't think about it, but a large amount of intangible assets never get monetized (converted to money). For example, coupons, "points" from various retailers (airlines, credit cards, and hotels), unused gift cards, etc. often never are used by individuals. These intangible assets can have value, but only if you use it to reduce planned spending and not just to buy items that you don't need.

GOVERNMENT AND TAXES

In 2015 the total spending by the United States federal, state and local government entities is slightly more than $6 trillion. Most of this spending is funded from taxes (including fees, permits, fines, licenses, etc.) on U.S. corporations and their citizens. Six Trillion Dollars or $6,000,000,000,000! Staggering isn't it. My guess is by 2050 this amount will double to $12,000,000,000,000 or Twelve Trillion Dollars!

So, unless you become part of the black and shadowy markets that operate out of the main stream, you need to understand that **proficient savers learn how to minimize what they pay to government and maximize what they get from government.** Clearly the people who have gotten the most money out of government are those citizens who are employed by government. On the other hand, the people who have minimized what they pay to government are high net worth individuals and the corporations that they lead. I could easily vilify both communities. Instead I applaud them. Both communities have learned the fine art of having government work in their interests while convincing others that government is actually interested in some ideologically common good that benefits all citizens.

For example, all governments, including the U.S., are particularly adept at providing numerous price subsidies for various products and services. Where it makes sense, you need to learn to take advantage of these subsidies. However, you also need to be extremely cautious since many subsidies have political incentives that are not in your best interests. Although many subsidies are inefficient and may make no economic sense this is not your concern, especially during the next decade. If a government subsidy benefits you, then use it to improve your overall financial well being.

The U.S. federal, state and local income tax regulations reflect one of many ways that governments reward the interests of those with the greatest lobbying power. It's another example of where policy is never fair because every benefactor defines fairness in their own selfish interests. If you can weave your way through the complexity there are numerous ways, which are constantly changing, where you can reap financial benefit. However, at the same time, you need to be cautious that the perceived value of certain benefits may handcuff your flexibility in the future.

Today, one of the greatest perks that the U.S. government provides to its citizens is the relative ease that students (and their parents) can borrow money to pay for a college education. Borrowers trade off the certainty of future debt repayments against the uncertainty of future wages (and other spending obligations). If borrowers do a poor job assessing their future career paths, then this benefit turns quickly into a liability that will anchor most borrowers until their death. Remember, many government handouts come with various conditions which usually require some form of repayment, or other form of concession, sometime in the future.

You also begin to realize the U.S. federal income tax system, which is highly progressive, is reaching deeper into the pockets of our society's most productive workers. Many of these workers are not rich and with the increasing burden of federal and state income taxes on wages never will be. However, when you begin to recognize that the federal income tax on taxable income of $100,000 is 28% and long term realized gains on wealth are taxed at 15% you have a better appreciation why accumulating savings is so important to your ability to achieve long term financial prosperity.

INVESTING WITH WISDOM

WHY
"INVESTING"
IS NOT WHAT
YOU THINK
IT IS.

DO YOU WANT TO BE RICH?

Similar to any question, your first query back to me should be, "Hmm ... how do you define Rich?" Well, not surprising, at least for the next several minutes, I want you to think of "Rich" strictly in financial terms. Therefore, my definition of "Rich" is as follows: A person is rich if they have sufficient resources to live the lifestyle they want into perpetuity; that is, until death. As you know from our discussions earlier, resources include tangible assets that you own (i.e. money, physical property and similar investments) and intangible assets that you possess (i.e. skills which I commonly refer to as K.I.T.E. — Knowledge, Insight, Technique and Experience).

In other words, using my definition, a rich person is, in a relative sense, financially independent. I want you to be rich; my hope is you have a similar desire. Also, I want you to be rich today, not tomorrow, with the probability of you staying rich increasing over time. Traditionally, many individuals believe those with income or wealth in the top 1% are rich and people who are retired are rich. Well, some are, and some aren't. Soon you will understand why.

CREATE AN ANNUITY

To become rich you need to create an annuity. An annuity is any resource that pays you money. If the annuity is sufficient to pay for your lifestyle over your remaining life; then you are rich. Let's take a simple example. Suppose the only asset you have is $200,000 in cash insured by the U.S. Federal Deposit Insurance Corporation ("FDIC"). You have five years to live and the lifestyle you enjoy costs $40,000 per year. Well, you are rich; that is you are financially independent because you have sufficient resources to live the way you want until you die. In a practical sense you cannot become richer. That is, if you die sooner, or your lifestyle costs decrease, you could make your heirs rich (or, a designated charity richer). On the other hand, if you live longer and the entity you depend on for your annuity defaults, or your lifestyle costs increase you can become poor. I would suggest you don't want to be poor.

WILL YOU BE WEALTHY?

The difference between being wealthy and rich, is that the wealthy have minimal risk of depleting their resources before they die. With respect to financial independence the wealthiest people are those who create an endowment that earns sufficient returns to pay their annual lifestyle expenses. For example, let's assume you are now 55 years old, your lifestyle expenses are $40,000 per year and current mortality tables would suggest you will live to be 85 years old. If you invest $1 million in a 30-year U.S. Treasury Bond that pays 4% interest per year, then you will generate sufficient monies to pay your annual living expenses. If you die at age 85, the $1 million will either pass to your heirs or to a charity. Although it is possible for you, and your peers to be rich, it is difficult, as you can imagine, to become wealthy. Between now and age 40, I want you to work on becoming rich. If you are rich at age 40, then we can discuss the pros and cons of becoming wealthy at age 50.

HOW TO THINK ABOUT RETIREMENT

In *Getting to 30* I introduced the concept of Lifetime Earnings and how much of your income you need to save for retirement. I imagined an individual who entered the workforce at age 25, retired at age 55 and died when they were 85 years old. In such a scenario, one would need, on average, an equal relationship between what they spent and what they saved to enjoy their retirement years.

For example, if you made $50,000 per year, your lifetime earnings would be $1.5 million. Since your lifetime earnings need to pay for your next sixty years of living, you could spend, on average, $25,000 each year. Since you have no earnings after age 55, you would need $750,000 in the bank to pay for your retirement. In other words, if the years you work equal the years you are retired, then you need to save 50% of your lifetime earnings. Now, I'm sure you noticed I did not complicate this simple model with hypothetical assumptions of investment returns and inflation expectations (remember, inflation impacts what you earn as well as what you buy). If it makes you feel better, assume the impact of investment returns and inflation essentially cancel each other out. This will keep things clear with the added benefit of sending most financial planners packing before they have an opportunity to dazzle you with their brilliance.

This model points out some obvious conclusions. If you plan to work less, then you need to save more and visa versa. That is, given the same level of income and spending, if you retire for 40 years and work 20 years, then you need to save twice as much, which of course would require an unrealistic savings rate equal to 100% of your income. On the other hand, if you work for 40 years and retire for

20 years, then you would only need to save 25% of your lifetime earnings.

In *Getting to 30*, I set a target savings rate of 25% of your income. It was a pretty daunting task and not surprising most of you did not, or have not, achieved this benchmark. Therefore, I have some good news for you. For the next 10 years don't think about a target savings rate for retirement. There isn't one! In fact, don't even think about retirement. Retirement is no longer the end game. If you follow the guidelines in this book and embrace the overall ideology of *Getting to 40*, I am confident you won't have to worry about having sufficient resources to retire in acceptable comfort. But don't fret. In Getting to 50 we will consider developing and fine tuning your retirement plan. Until then, forget about it.

So, if you're not saving for retirement, then why are you saving? Well, you save now for two primary reasons. First, to provide yourself the greatest flexibility during the next ten years. Second, to minimize, if possible your future occupancy costs. Consequently, your two biggest investment assets during your 30s will be cash and your home. I like to think of it as a barbell investment strategy where you hold super safe "liquid" cash in half of your investment portfolio and in the other half you hold relatively "illiquid" equity that is invested in your home. The sides of the barbell, however, will never be perfectly balanced since there always will be a slight tilt in one direction or another. This two-prong barbell strategy also provides a nice hedge in a volatile environment where it is difficult to know the direction of future prices. That is, cash becomes more valuable in a deflationary environment and your home should become more valuable in an inflationary environment.

The point is, you should maintain the principal control of your assets, just like taking control of your career.

Maybe this sounds a bit boring, but you will find contentment in an investment strategy that is predictable and minimizes surprises during a period of time where your primary focus will be on your career.

Your home is essentially an investment in real estate. Real estate will be the cornerstone of your investment philosophy throughout your life. Therefore, I will spend a bit of time making sure you thoroughly understand the benefits and pitfalls of investing in real estate. However, before I do this, let's take a moment and review why it's a bad idea to use debt (i.e. leverage) as part of your overall investment philosophy.

THERE IS NO "GOOD" DEBT

A person born in January 1992, who incurred $1,000 in credit card debt on his 18th birthday in January 2010, would owe $81,785 when he retired at age 68; assuming an annual interest rate of only 20% and that he let the initial obligation and the interest accrue for fifty years. Oh, the magic of compound interest.

What's interesting, of course, is financial advisors always use such a scenario to discuss your assets, but never your debt. So, let's take a couple of minutes and summarize some of the key points I made regarding debt in *Getting to 30*. As you can probably tell, if K.I.T.E. is one of my favorite 4-letter words then DEBT is probably the one I hate the most (even more than the F*** word).

You should never (except in very rare instances) borrow money to make an investment. Moreover, if you have debt, you should always (except in very rare instances) use any excess cash to pay off debt (especially credit card debt).

People who borrow money to invest believe they can create wealth through the use of arbitrage and leverage.

Experts might. You can't. Arbitrage is the difference between what you earn on an investment and the interest you pay to borrow the money. Leverage is the relationship between the amount of money you borrow to invest and the amount of personal savings you invest. If you have no personal savings (i.e. no net worth), then ALL of your investments are from borrowed funds. If all of your investments are from borrowed funds, then there is a very high likelihood you are destroying wealth by actually going deeper in debt.

Arbitrage and leverage are actually purely mathematical concepts. For example, suppose you want to invest $10,000 in a particular stock. You believe (based on conversations with numerous experts) this stock will return 10% during the next year. Since you only have $2,000 in savings, you decide to borrow $8,000 on a home equity line of credit. The bank decides to charge you 4% for this loan. If your prediction turns out to be correct, then the return on your equity savings is a whopping 34%. The return is a function of the amount of arbitrage (that is, 6%; the investment earns 10% and you pay the bank 4%) multiplied by the amount of leverage (that is 4; $8,000 of borrowed funds divided by $2,000 of your savings). In other words, you earned 24% more on your investment then the "unleveraged" return of 10%.

The mistake all rookie investors (whoops; I mean speculators) make is they assume the risk of the investment is comparable to the risk of the borrowed funds. This is clearly not the case. If this was true, then a creditor would charge you an interest rate that was comparable to the actual risk that you are taking on the investment. That is, there would be no arbitrage.

Novice investors make this mistake all the time. Typically, what they learn the hard way is the true risk of the investment will manifest itself in the volatility of returns (the slam dunk stock investment actually loses 10%) and then all of the sudden the returns go in reverse and the losses balloon; sometimes exponentially. In other words, a 10% loss now results in negative arbitrage of 14% (you lost 10% and paid the bank 4%) multiplied by the amount of leverage. After you liquidate your loan, your original savings of $2,000 is now reduced to $680 (i.e. investment loss of $1,000 and interest paid of $320) or an investment loss of 66%. In other words, the negative arbitrage of 14% coupled with the leverage of 4 is a loss of 56% which magnifies the actual unleveraged investment loss that was only 10%.

It will always make sense to pay off the mortgage on your home as soon as possible. It will never make sense to "borrow" the equity in your home and invest it with the hope of earning more on your investments than the interest cost on your debt. If it did, then why would you ever make a downpayment on your home or a principal payment on your debt?

You need to remember all financial advisors and investment funds are compensated based on either the assets you invest or the investment trades you make. That is, their focus is on the left side of your balance sheet (not the right side which shows your net worth and debt). Sadly, because of their unwavering belief in positive arbitrage, in their mind, the more debt you have, the better. The difference between their guidance and my advice is that I actually care about your interests, not theirs.

As you know, many people borrow for their education, which has the potential (if done judiciously) to provide a reasonable return on investment. However, student loan debt is actually the most insidious debt of all because, except in very rare cases, this debt can not be eliminated in bankruptcy. Moreover, the federal government can garnish your wages, collect your income tax refund and even withhold a portion of your Social Security retirement.

Consequently, student loan debt can easily become legacy debt. It will shackle many people in your generation until death; especially for those individuals who make very poor career decisions. Sadly, student loan debt reflects the curse of easy borrowing where often the advisors have significant conflicts of interest (i.e. university financial aid personnel) and career counselors (i.e. parents, teachers, friends, etc.) who provide terrible advice and/or support a student's poor decisions.

Most individuals who turn 30 with a significant amount of student debt (i.e. greater than $100,000 in 2015) will have a difficult time achieving financial freedom. In many cases, they have difficult career trade-offs if they pursue government programs that provide various forms of debt forgiveness. However, perhaps the worst part of student debt (like all debt) is that you lose the flexibility to pursue the career you love because now you need to earn money primarily to pay off an obligation you hate. It's another reminder why it's difficult to achieve financial freedom at age 40 if individuals make poor decisions *Getting to 30*. **If you're tethered to debt in your 30s you will never earn money doing what you love.**

WHY CASH IS YOUR BEST ASSET

During the next 10 years, your key asset is cash. It is key because you will use cash for two primary reasons:

- Avoid Debt
- Invest in your Career

The most important reason to have sufficient levels of cash (held in a relatively safe FDIC insured bank account) is to ensure stability, especially in times of crisis. However, cash not only makes it possible to fund emergencies but also to invest in opportunities that will enhance your career. Moreover, as you will see, cash reserves serve many other very useful purposes. However, the primary reason to hold cash is to avoid debt. Credit is seldom available in times of financial distress and when it is the cost of such debt is usurious. As you will learn, your ability to avoid paying interest on debt is more powerful, and more important, than the return you might earn on leveraged investments.

Your goal is to build this emergency fund to an amount equal to your projected spending for the coming year. For example, if you spend $75,000 in 2015, then your cash reserves should be no less than $75,000 on January 1, 2016. In addition to minimizing the risk of going in debt, holding cash, whose primary value is liquidity, has many additional advantages, including:

- Savings Discipline — the reason you see a proliferation of government savings vehicles is that politicians believe individuals will not save without such incentives. Therefore, when money is locked away in relatively illiquid investments, it is very difficult to tap these funds for immediate gratification. If you are going to achieve financial independence you must have the discipline to save. Building your cash reserves and then replenishing these reserves when needed will help you develop this discipline.

- Investment Returns — one of the primary reasons individuals suffer poor returns on long-term retirement investments, like stock index funds, is because of their need to take money out of their retirement fund and then replenish it in the future. In other words, their monies never stay invested for the long term because they are constantly withdrawing cash for emergency and other needs. This relentless churning often leads to a buy-high, sell-low investment behavior and increased fees and other expenses. You cannot invest for the long term until you have sufficient cash reserves to fund emergency and other unexpected scenarios. Seek safety now and you will have greater flexibility to seek "discipline" risk in the future.

• An Option for Tomorrow — cash doesn't yield a return but it can be priceless when it comes to taking advantage of future opportunities. After you build sufficient reserves, cash is still valuable because it will help you buy assets when markets turn them into bargains. There is nothing more valuable to a desperate seller than a buyer who can pay in cash. Things which appear pricey today have a reasonably good chance of declining in value in the future. Always remember, cash is a very precious commodity, especially to those who don't have it.

• Insurance Against Risks — just like buying insurance before your house burns down, your car hits a deer, or your health deteriorates, cash is your insurance against unexpected and unfavorable future economic events.

• Hedge Against Deflation — the more discretionary spending you have, the greater your ability to take advantage of seasonal sales or other anticipated price declines. In addition, many vendors will offer additional discounts if you pay "early." The best way to take advantage of possible future price declines is to hoard cash and then to have the patience to deploy it judiciously. Remember, especially in a deflationary environment, cash will always "rise" in value.

- Arbitrage Credit Costs — Today, a typical credit card transaction (or other "borrowing" transaction) will cost a seller (of products or services) between 2% and 3% of the retail price. Because this cost is essentially passed on to a buyer, you should be able to negotiate a discount, especially for large purchases, if you pay cash. Although the supply chain is becoming flatter, a typical credit transaction requires communication among a half-dozen organizations (billing processor, card association like VISA/Master Card, your bank, the retailer's bank, a payment processor, the clearing house network, etc.). Paying cash is the best way to eliminate the escalating fees associated with a credit transaction.

- Career Opportunities — there is nothing worse than being trapped in a career you hate because you cannot "afford" to make a career change that would greater enhance your future opportunities. Cash provides you the flexibility to absorb significant moving expenses, a reduction in salary (replaced with contingent bonuses or future stock options), pay for training or new skills, or to fund part of the start up costs of a new business venture.

Keep in mind your generation is entering an environment where there is a greater likelihood future annual growth rates (and therefore long-term investment returns) will not exceed 3%. In addition, there is the real possibility all of us are entering a world where governments and central banks will battle deflation on an ongoing basis. In such an environment, where uncertainty and volatility rule the day, cash is even more valuable. Invest in cash and then embrace returns that value choice and flexibility.

REAL ESTATE — YOUR BEST LONG TERM INVESTMENT

In *Getting to 30*, I devoted an entire chapter to buying a home. The general theme five years ago was owning your own home: free of debt. Today's theme: make a great investment. Real estate is your best long term asset and your home will be your first real estate investment. If you don't own your home yet, there is a strong likelihood you will in the next 10 years. As a result, it's important that we revisit this topic with some new views on the pros and cons of owning your home.

For most people, the cost of shelter is their greatest individual fixed cost, whether measured in absolute dollars, a percentage of their monthly expenses or a percentage of their annual net wages. If you buy a home, your objective should be to minimize your cost of shelter relative to the money you would have

The process of buying a home is similar to any investment decision.

spent to rent your shelter. Although the purchase of a home should enhance your quality of life, you cannot let your emotions override sound economic decision making. If you make a wise decision, then you will have the cornerstone of a strong foundation as you move along your path to financial independence.

For most people in their 30s it will be the most important investment decision during their relatively short lifetime. If you decide to buy a home, your home will be your most significant asset. However, even if you rent, your home is the infrastructure that facilitates your lifestyle and quality of life. It can have a tremendous impact with respect to the success of your family, the development of your skills and your productivity at work. However, if you are "house poor" because you spend too much money relative to your income it will be the primary cause of your financial stress and eventually your financial demise.

How Much Should You Spend On Shelter?

How much money you spend for your shelter, of course, will depend on your wants, needs and other preferences. However, in my opinion, you will not achieve financial independence unless your total cost of shelter stays below 24% of your gross wages. If you rent, then your total cost of shelter will include the cash you pay to your landlord, the amount you pay for utilities and insurance for your personal items. If you own your home, then the total cost of shelter will include the interest you pay to your lender, the amount you pay for utilities, homeowner's insurance, real estate taxes, and general maintenance. In today's market, the estimated costs of owning a home is approximately 12% of a home's value. Therefore, the maximum value you should pay for any home should not exceed two times your gross wages. For example, if your gross wages are $75,000 a year, then your maximum shelter costs should not exceed $18,000 a year, or $1,500 a month. The maximum value you should pay for a home should not exceed $150,000.

The total cost of your shelter should not exceed 24% of your gross wages and the value of your home should not exceed two times your gross wages.

Many people tell me they want to buy a home because they hate "throwing away money on rent". What most people don't understand is that they either rent their shelter or they "rent" the money to buy their shelter. That is, all of the costs that a landlord incurs and passes on to you, well for the most part, you will incur essentially the same costs if you owned the place instead of renting it. The only difference is the landlord tacks on an additional amount to compensate themselves for their costs and risks of leasing a home (major repairs, bad tenants, administrative costs, lack of liquidity, bank financing, etc.). The elimination of the landlord's return is the primary reason individuals can usually, for exactly the same amount of dollars, buy a nicer home than they can rent.

Understanding the Cost of Shelter

To help you better understand, let's take a moment and break down the total costs of shelter. As I noted above, the annual cost of owning a home in today's market is approximately 12% of a home's value. How does the 12% breakdown? Well, 4% is interest paid to the bank; 4% is utilities; 2.5% is real estate taxes; .5% is insurance and 1% is a general reserve for maintenance and other unforeseen expenses.

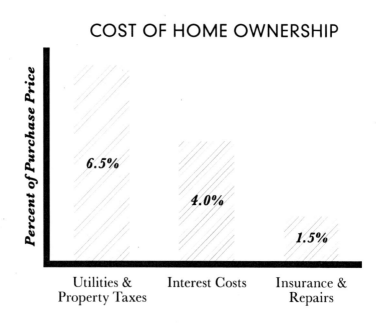

COST OF HOME OWNERSHIP

Percent of Purchase Price

6.5%

4.0%

1.5%

Utilities & Property Taxes   Interest Costs   Insurance & Repairs

The costs of ownership can be higher if you buy a "comparable" condominium instead of a "freestanding" home because you lose control of many of the variable expenses which are then bundled with a management fee and billed to you in a monthly homeowners association fee. The only fixed cost in this model is the cost of interest. All of the other costs are variable costs, which you should expect to increase in the future.

If you rent an identical home, the only difference is the 4% interest will morph into a 10% unleveraged return to the landlord, so a $150,000 house should cost $2,250 a month to rent and $1,500 to "own." You should think of this relative difference as your mobility premium. Market forces might squeeze this difference but it would be rare for it to be eliminated entirely. In situations where the cost of home ownership is more than the cost to rent there is a reasonably good chance that home values are too high and a collapse in values will eventually occur.

You will notice I don't include any principal repayment of your loan as a "cost" of your home. The interest you incur on your mortgage impacts the cost of your home. The principal amount you borrow to buy your home does not. That is, **the value of your home does not change regardless of how you choose to finance it.** You could buy your home for no money down or I could pay cash for the same home. In either scenario, the price paid for the home would be the same. As discussed earlier, you cannot change (increase or decrease) the value of an asset based on how you choose to pay for the asset (equity or debt).

When you pay off the principal on your home mortgage all you do is exchange one asset in your portfolio (cash) for another asset (equity in your home). Except for avoiding negative interest arbitrage (which I will discuss later), there is no value creation in this exchange. You will still have an "opportunity cost of capital" (that is, interest you could earn on the "money" invested in your house). However, this "opportunity cost" will always be less than the interest cost that you would pay on a mortgage. This conclusion assumes relatively stable prices. If home prices were increasing or decreasing significantly (massive inflation or tremendous deflation) this conclusion may or may not hold depending on numerous other factors. However, as we have discussed on a number of occasions, owing no debt is always beneficial, especially in periods of significant price volatility.

As you digest the above cost components, the first item you will recognize is that utility costs related to your basic shelter, primarily delivered by various government or quasi-government entities, are increasing substantially, especially in many parts of the country. Utility costs include expenses principally related to water, heat (gas, electric, propane, etc.), sewer, and waste disposal.

More and more, the cost of "living" in your home exceeds the cost of buying your home.

These costs can easily exceed the interest rate you pay on your mortgage. That is, on a $150,000 home you should expect your annual utility costs will approximate $6,000 a month, or 4% of the home's value.

Moreover, the identical situation is true for escalating real estate taxes (which often include utility related costs as well as costs related to the local school systems, libraries, metro parks, zoos, sports stadiums, municipal services, child services, mental health services, disabled citizens, etc.).

Politicians like to emphasize the interest expense component when they talk about the cost and affordability of housing. In fact, the cost of utilities and real estate taxes not only exceed the interest cost component but often the landlord returns in many rental situations. Unfortunately, the unfavorable trends in utilities and real estate costs during the past 20 years are going to continue for two primary reasons. First, the infrastructure involved in the delivery of water, gas, electricity and waste management is old. Second, the pension plans for retired municipal workers, school teachers and other government employees are significantly underfunded. The cost to maintain and/or replace aging infrastructure and the costs to pay these retirees are going to be borne directly by the homeowner or indirectly by the tenants.

The other unfavorable trend is the cost of insurance. Severe weather events (tornados, hurricanes, floods, wildfires etc.) and natural catastrophes (earthquakes, landslides, sinkholes, etc.) are occurring more frequently. Traditionally, individuals would pay approximately .5% of a home's value for insurance, or $750 on a $150,000 investment. These costs are not only increasing, but policies have more exclusions, riders to insure specific risks and higher deductibles. Consequently, homeowners who live in areas of greater risk are bearing higher insurance costs for such decisions (exceeding 1% of a home's value in some situations). This trend will probably continue unless insurance companies can convince their other policy holders to subsidize the potential losses of those who live in more dangerous areas. In other words, the risks of where you live are shifting more directly to the homeowner and the tenant.

You will bear these costs either directly as a homeowner or indirectly as a renter (if you rent and the landlord pays such costs, then the landlord will pass such costs on to you in the form of higher rent).

Where you live determines what you pay, not only today, but even more importantly, in the future. You need to be diligent in keeping your total cost of shelter below 24% of your gross wages and your home investment no more than two times your gross wages (primarily because you want to maintain a high degree of flexibility to take advantage of career opportunities that might require you to move). You must conserve energy and proactively manage your utility costs. It's important you understand the impact of weather related risks on where you live (fire, floods, mudslides, hurricanes, tornados, etc.). Perhaps you need to share your shelter with others or lower your expectations of your dream home. What you should not do is let others persuade you to breach these thresholds.

Should You Buy or Rent Your Shelter?

From a purely economic perspective you should buy your shelter if the cost of owning your shelter will be less than the cost of renting your shelter. In theory, a home can be a great investment because it has the potential to minimize the cost of your shelter over your lifetime. In general, the longer you live in your home, the better the investment, because you avoid some of the costs you would have to pay to rent your shelter in the future.

What most people do not understand, is **the minute you move into your home you have negative equity** because your house will be worth less than you paid for it. Why? Because transaction costs will chew away at your net worth while tremendously benefiting other players in the home ownership supply chain. Time is the only variable that will help you eliminate this deficit. In other words, every homeowner hopes their home will appreciate enough to at least justify the costs of buying and financing their house. Transaction costs fall into three basic baskets of expenses.

Basket #1 is the cost paid to the real estate company as a sales commission.

Basket #2 are the costs paid for due diligence and include inspections, home warranty, surveys, flood certification, title insurance, title search, attorney fees, conveyance fees, recording fees and other costs to complete the transaction.

Basket #3 are the costs you incur to secure a mortgage (i.e. for monies you borrow from a bank or other lender to buy the house) and includes escrow fees, loan origination costs, loan discount points, credit reports, application fees, underwriting fee, lender's title insurance.

Similar to other costs of homeownership (utilities, real estate taxes and insurance) transaction costs can vary significantly from location to location. However, in general, real estate commissions approximate 6% of the purchase price; due diligence 2%; and mortgage fees 2%. Therefore, total transaction costs on a home approximate 10% of the purchase price. Many home buyers, especially first-time home buyers, are not aware of the magnitude of these costs because they are summarized and buried on complex closing cost worksheets. These worksheets are usually prepared by the title company based on input from the bankers and real estate agents.

Therefore, if you buy a home and then decide you need to move during the next year, you will most likely incur a loss of 10% on the value of the home. That is, if you purchase a home for $150,000 and sell it for $150,000 your loss is $15,000. In fact, there is a pretty good likelihood your loss is even greater because there will always be duplicate costs you pay when you buy and when you sell. As you can easily see, the more you buy and sell (which is often referred to as "churn"), the more the benefits of home ownership accrue to the transaction players and not to the homeowner.

Consequently, before you buy a home, it is important for you to assess mobility risk (the likelihood you may need to change locations to obtain a new job). There are five primary ways to minimize mobility risk. First, you can pursue opportunities that will provide you with relatively stable sources of future income. Second, you can locate in a large metropolitan area that has many possible job opportunities that match your career objectives. Third, you can purchase a home in a stable neighborhood with high resale possibilities. Fourth, you can lower your expectations for your dream home. Fifth, you can try to tap competent friends and family (e.g. primarily as inspectors, lawyers, lenders and financial advisors) to assist in the home purchase process for the sole purpose of reducing your transaction costs.

The greatest risk when you buy a home is that you might have to move.

Here are my rough guidelines to minimize mobility risk. First, never buy a home unless there is a reasonable chance you will live in the home for at least two years. Second, do not buy a home unless the cost of ownership is projected to be substantially less than the amount you would have paid in rent (i.e. your break-even point) in a worst case scenario.

Here is one example on how to go through this thought process. You and your spouse make $100,000 per year. You currently rent a two-bedroom townhouse in an up-scale suburb in a nice midwestern city for total shelter costs of $2,000 a month. Because you assess mobility risk as high, you decide to lower your expectations of your dream house and locate a relatively small 1,500 square foot home in nice stable neighborhood that you agree to purchase for $150,000. Fortunately you have lots of friends. Friend #1, a local real estate agent, agrees to reduce his real estate commission when you sell to 5%. Friend #2, a local lawyer, agrees to manage the entire due diligence process for 1.5% of the sales price. Friend #3, a local mortgage broker, agrees all lender closing costs will not exceed 1.5% of the purchase price. You take a deep breath knowing your transaction costs have been reduced to 8%. During the due diligence process you noticed real estate taxes have been capped at 2% (obviously you are not buying a home in Cleveland!); the home has natural gas and therefore total utility costs should approximate 3.5%; and because the home is relatively new you do not expect any major maintenance costs. Therefore, your total projected annual shelter cost after the purchase is 10% of value (i.e. interest 4%; utilities 3.5%; real estate taxes 2% and .5% for insurance). Sure enough, after two years you and your spouse receive a great offer to move to the sunny south. Your projections hold and you sell your house for $150,000. Whew! Well, did you make a good financial decision? Let's see.

Your direct cost of shelter was $30,000 for the two years (i.e. $150,000 x 10% x 2 years). In addition, the transaction costs you paid on your home was $12,000 (i.e. $150,000 x 8%). Therefore, your total cost of shelter for the two years was $42,000. If you would have stayed in your two bedroom townhouse your total shelter costs would have been $48,000 (i.e. $2,000 x 24 months). So, in this scenario you made a good

The benefits of home ownership increase as mobility risk declines.

decision even with high mobility risk. You paid $42,000 to live in a nice home in a nice suburb versus $48,000 to rent a two-bedroom townhouse. A savings of $6,000. Consequently, your total shelter costs averaged 21% of gross wages, slightly below the maximum suggested threshold of 24%. But, it was close call. A minor change in variables, for example the inability to sell your home quickly, and the "savings" you achieved could have easily evaporated; poof!

Due Diligence — Buyer Beware

If you decide to purchase a home, you need to hire competent independent professionals to assist you in your due diligence process. Under no circumstances should you trust any of the representations made by the seller or any other individual involved in the transaction process (e.g. builders, real estate agents, bankers, mortgage brokers, title company representatives, etc.). You should understand even written representations and contracts mean little in today's environment. Sellers, along with their real estate agents and bankers, will participate in outright fraud by not disclosing what they know. This includes defects, often caused by builders and shoddy contractors, that have been purposely hidden from the buyer.

Trust your instincts, draw on the expertise of friends and families, and always be willing to walk away from a transaction where something doesn't feel right. Although you may have legal recourse against the seller after closing, seldom will the benefit of litigation exceed the cost of a lawsuit (including the time you will spend pursuing it). Even if you win a lawsuit against the builder or previous homeowner, there is a pretty strong likelihood they will not have the resources to pay the damages that they owe to you.

Just in the last year, I had sellers misrepresent the ownership of the land's mineral rights, fill in a small pond and hide it with a new gazebo, put paneling up in a basement over a major structural problem, paint over black mold, hide defective wall board, not disclose major drain backup issues, lie about a fence that was on someone else's property, forget about a major assessment for a new sewer, provide fake invoices for services that were never performed, clean a rug whose underlying padding had been destroyed with dog feces and cat piss, sign off that defective electrical wiring was consistent with existing building codes, ignore the lack of insulation in the walls and ceiling, and sadly I could go on and on.

As you get older, you will truly be amazed at the length sellers will go through to put "lipstick on a pig." Moreover, even if there is a homeowner's association, seldom are the rules actively enforced and often there is significant deferred maintenance (especially true with condo associations) that will require a major increase in future dues and assessments. In addition, most cities that require permits and inspections do so solely to create fee revenues. In most cases city inspectors have no idea what they are looking at and there is no accountability to the homebuyer and no consequence to the city employee for poor performance.

In addition to rising property tax and utility bills you will also experience the unbundling of costs and direct billing of expenses (broken water mains, damaged sidewalks, cracked sewer pipes, waste disposal, etc.) related specifically to the property you own. What these costs are today and how they will trend in the future will be directly related to where you live. Traditionally, these costs have been a minor part of due diligence during the home buying process. Unless you want unwelcome surprises that will blow your budget, it is critical you understand these costs, and the government that controls them, before you consummate the purchase of your home.

Finally, canvas the neighborhood. Sometimes your new neighbors will provide you the most interesting insights. Pay particular notice to the number of for sale signs, houses for rent, unkept lawns, property that looks like a salvage yard and other indicators of an unstable neighborhood. Review the demographics of your neighborhood, the quality of the public school system, crime statistics and the depth and breadth of public services. If the neighborhood is not nice today, it is unlikely it will be in the future.

In today's environment, you can not approach the due diligence process with a cavalier attitude. Your lack of attention to detail will cost you thousands of dollars you will never recover. It's important you do everything possible to protect your most significant financial investment. No one else will! Buy your home based on what you know is true, not based on a hope, a dream or the marketing prowess of conflicted representatives.

What Is The Right Downpayment?

You should put down the most funds possible while maintaining a high degree of comfort you will not need to take on additional debt, especially credit card debt, during the term of the mortgage. If you cannot amortize your mortgage in 15 years or less you probably are buying too nice of a home based on the amount of money you make and your overall financial condition. Based on today's metrics, and assuming you are at the maximum payment threshold for your cost of shelter, you will have to make a downpayment equal to approximately 8% of the purchased price in order to qualify for a Federal Housing Administration ("FHA") mortgage. In most cases if you you don't meet FHA guidelines the bank will not loan you the money.

Financial advisors who advocate thirty-year mortgage repayment terms want you to buy into a concept known as positive interest arbitrage ("+IA"). In fact, if you really believe in this concept, your home loan would be interest only. Moreover, you would borrow additional funds to the extent you had any increase in your home's value to ensure 100% of your home's value was always owed to a third party. The three largest mortgage lenders in the U.S., Wells Fargo, Bank of America and J.P. Morgan Chase market these interest only (usually with a maturity of up to ten years) as Home Equity Lines of Credit or HELOC. So here's a bit of common sense. **If someone loans you 100% of the value of your home, well guess what, you don't "own" your home. The bank does!**

In Reality, "Pure" +IA Isn't Possible. Why?

+IA occurs when you earn more on an investment than the interest you paid on the funds that were used to acquire the investment. That is, if you paid 4% interest a year on a $150,000 mortgage, then your home, as an investment, would need to appreciate 4% a year to break-even. However, if inflation was projected to be in excess of 4% a year, then you would not be able to obtain a 4% interest rate on your mortgage.

The way bankers and other interested parties convince you of +IA is by substituting high risk and volatile investments for your low risk home that tends to maintain a relatively stable value over time. For example, if you invest in iShares PFF today you would receive a dividend of 6.5%. +IA is 2.5% a year when compared to the 4% interest paid on your mortgage. However, you have two unknowns related to your PFF investment. First, will the current dividend be higher or lower than the 6.5% in the future? Second, will the value of the PFF investment show a gain or loss ten years from now?

Both of these risks need to be compared to a known scenario. That is, a mortgage that requires an interest payment equal to 4% of principal and matures (or resets with a new interest rate and amortization schedule) 10 years from now. The investment risk of the unknown is not comparable to the liability risk of the known. In other words, no astute investor is going to allow you to borrow $150,000 for 10 years at 4% interest per year and invest those funds in PFF shares, collateralized only by the shares.

If +IA is not possible, then the only alternative is negative interest arbitrage ("-IA"). **The primary reason you want to pay off your mortgage as soon as possible is to avoid negative interest arbitrage.** The longer you pay, the more you pay, as the impact of -IA compounds over many years. In addition, if you rent a comparable home, instead of owning it, then -IA is now even worse because of the extra return you are paying to the landlord.

Let's see how this would work. Assume you can pay cash, if you want, for your home purchase. Scenario A: You purchase your home for $150,000 cash. Scenario B you purchase your home but the banker convinces you a 4% interest only HELOC for 10 years is the way to go. If this is the way to go today, then this is the way to go for your lifetime (which might last another 60 years — yea — you live to 90!) so you just keep rolling over this debt during your lifetime. However, because you are not positive the bank will rollover your debt every 10 years you invest your cash in a 10-year U.S. Treasury Note that earns 2% per year. Scenario C: You rent the same home for your lifetime and invest your cash in a 10-year U.S. Treasury Note. So, what happens?

Well, under Scenario A your total cost of shelter is 8% of the home's value (not the 12% mentioned earlier because you have no interest charge), or $12,000 per year. Under Scenario B your total cost of shelter is 10% of the home's value (i.e. 12% less the 2% you earn every year on your Treasury Note investment), or $15,000 per year. Under Scenario C your total cost of shelter is 16% of the home's value (i.e. 12% plus the 6% bonus paid to the landlord less 2% return on the U.S. Treasury Note), or $24,000 a year. Consequently, the cost of being in perpetual debt over your lifetime will require you to come up with an additional $180,000 while the cost to rent your shelter will require you to fork over an additional $720,000. Not a good path to financial independence.

What Is Your Real Interest Rate?

There are two variables that impact the actual effective interest rate you pay on your home. The first variable is the total amount of transaction costs that you pay to obtain your mortgage. The second variable is the possible tax benefit you could receive on the interest you pay. Both of these items are discussed below.

The only interest rate that matters when you finance your home's purchase is the annual percentage rate (APR). The APR is not the interest rate used to calculate your mortgage. APR is the interest rate you actually pay once you factor in all fees and other transaction costs. Let's take a very simple example.

If a mortgage broker quotes you 4% on a mortgage that requires 2 points to close (which is the same as a 2% transaction cost), then the actual cost of your mortgage is 4.08%. In simple terms, what this means, is that in order to "borrow" $150,000 you need to pay a fee of 2%, or $3,000. If you borrow $150,000 but only receive $147,000 (because it costs you $3,000 to receive $147,000), then the $6,000 you pay in interest payments is not based off a $150,000 loan; it is based on a $147,000 "mortgage".

The quickest way to calculate a rough approximation of the APR, is to multiply the interest rate for the mortgage by (1 + transaction cost percentage). In the above example, you would multiply 4% by (1 + 2%) = 4.08%. As discussed earlier, the financing transaction costs include all of the costs in Basket #3 (if it is a new purchase) and all transaction costs (Baskets #2 and Basket #3) if you are refinancing.

Mortgage brokers seldom calculate the APR correctly because they follow rote models that don't take into account all of the relevant costs. The best way to know the actual interest rate you are paying is to take all of the costs the broker expects you to pay and divide it by the money you expect to borrow (which is the price on your purchase agreement less your downpayment). This is the transaction percentage you should use to calculate your APR.

Calculating the "real" APR is the only way to compare the cost of competing offers for ANY financing (mortgage, car, credit cards). If you don't understand this concept and how brokers massage the numbers there is a high likelihood you will select the financing that actually has the highest cost.

The next variable impacting the actual interest rate you pay is the amount of any tax benefit you receive from the U.S. government to subsidize home ownership (all tax benefits subsidize something). The tax benefits you receive lower the effective cost of the interest you pay on your mortgage.

The rules governing the calculation of this benefit are complex (e.g. the discussions below assume you are filing your tax returns as a married couple in 2015). In general, for reasons discussed below, **the tax benefits you receive from financing your home should never impact the amount of your downpayment or the amount of your financing.** In other words, you should never buy a home because of the "tax benefits."

1. The tax benefits don't begin unless your interest payments exceed $12,600. In other words, assuming a 4% interest rate, a married couple's mortgage would need to exceed $315,000 (and even then, the benefit is only the amount of "itemized deductions" that exceed $12,600).

2. The tax benefits begin to phase out as wages increase. In 2015, this phase out begins for a married couple once their income exceeds $305,050. You should expect this phase out to continue and there is a strong likelihood that this "benefit" will be completely eliminated in your lifetime. As millennials you should understand that this benefit (which is actually quite minimal) is an indirect cost on all renters who prize mobility over the anchor of home ownership.

3. The tax benefit of the interest deduction does not impact interest arbitrage. In other words, to the extent you receive a benefit on the interest you pay you also pay a tax on the interest you earn with respect to most arbitrage strategies.

4. As mentioned earlier, the cost of living in your home now exceeds the cost of financing your home. Although you should minimize the cost of financing your home, your primary focus should be on the real costs of living in your home.

5. The most significant tax benefit of owning your home is that a married couple in 2015 can exclude a gain on the sale of their home up to $500,000. How you finance your home does not impact the calculation of this gain. Without question, long term home ownership in an area where real estate values are increasing would generate more benefit to you than any other tax deferred or tax free savings gimmicks.

If you're interested, *Getting to 30* goes more into the actual mathematics of the tax benefit of interest payments on your home. However, as noted above, any possible tax benefit only adds an unnecessary complexity to an already complex decision.

Understand What Drives a Home's Value

The price you pay for a home reflects the R~I~P~P~L~E~S of the local community. If a community has sufficient resources (a well diversified and highly educated workforce that lives or works in an area that has sufficient parks and recreation), sound infrastructure (public services, communications, transportation and healthcare), reasonable policies (those that support safety, building codes and taxes), competent leaders (working for the community and not themselves) and excellent education (strong public schools that embrace parental involvement), then there is a good chance the price you pay for your home today can be recovered when you sell your home in the future.

Earlier I stated you should live in your home no less than two years if you don't want to lose money. If you want to protect yourself, you should have a reasonable level of confidence you will be your home more than five years.

Next to mobility risk, the greatest risk to a homeowner is that they overpay for their home (based on their income or based on the market).

Whether your home actually appreciates beyond your investment (the price you paid and any permanent improvements you might make) is a very tricky question (which is actually true for ALL assets). If you move into a growing community, and hit the sweet spot when you sell (that is, community housing supply has not been able to keep up with demand) then consider yourself extremely lucky. This is not the norm and you should not anticipate this outcome. The best scenario is for the community to reach a nice equilibrium where there are relatively few homes for sale and most of the families intend to be in the communities for a long period of time. Changing demographics, however, can have a devastating impact on home values (large companies shut down, young families begin to leave or baby boomers start to downsize and beginning selling their homes). Moreover, the higher the price of your home, the more unique your home (style, location, landscaping, pets) and a large number of deferred maintenance projects will collectively reduce the number of interested buyers and put downward pressure on the value you will receive at the time you sell. I guess the point is you should buy your home first for lifestyle and second to minimize your cost of living. If it actually turns out to be a good investment, that is an added bonus.

Summary Comments on Home Ownership

A home is an investment because it allows you to minimize the cost of shelter over your lifetime. The longer you live in your home, the better the investment, because you avoid the costs you would have to pay to rent your shelter in the future. Therefore, the question is not if you should invest in a home; the question is when. Keep in mind, however, either you own your shelter, the bank "owns" your shelter or the landlord owns your shelter. Because the benefits of home ownership require, among other things, stability of your job and the stability of your community, it is often difficult for many homeowners to capture this value.

Astute finance majors, and other professionals, will argue you should borrow as much as you can and ramp up the risk of your investments to maximize +IA. In other words, let's anchor our need for stable day to day shelter for our family to the high risk returns and volatility of emerging markets. Really? Does this make any sense? Yet this is the type of nonsense that perpetuates in everyday discussions with financial advisors. Instead, minimize -IA by paying off your mortgage as quickly as possible.

Your total cost of shelter must be less than 24% of your current gross wages. As discussed above, cost of shelter does not include money used to repay the principal portion of any debt. Over time the fixed financing cost (i.e. interest expense) should be reduced to zero which should help minimize the pain of increasing variable costs related to living in your home (i.e. utilities, real estate taxes, insurance, maintenance and repairs). Moreover, if your wages increase then the cost of living in your home should become a smaller percentage of your total fixed costs. If you cannot afford an 8% downpayment and believe a 15-year principal amortizing loan will breach the FHA mortgage guidelines, then you need to buckle down on your savings and lower your expectations of what type of home you can afford.

AVOID THE GOVERNMENT SAVINGS NUDGE

As you probably have learned by now, the Internal Revenue Service, under the auspices of the U.S. Federal Government, has developed numerous vehicles to help you to save for retirement. These vehicles typically go by the name of the IRS code section such as 401(k), 403(b), 457(b), IRA, Roth IRA, H.R. 10, Keogh, SIMPLE, SEP, and the most recent attempt by the government to encourage retirement saving, the myRA. In addition, there are other government plans that entice you to save for future health care costs or college costs for your kids.

In order to nudge you to save for retirement, THE IRS (not surprising, when combined into one word you get THEIRS) generally allows you to avoid paying taxes on certain wages today with an understanding you will pay a tax on these wages when you withdraw them for retirement. Moreover, investment earnings on wages that are not taxed today (i.e. before tax contributions) or contributions of wages that already have been taxed (i.e. after tax dollars) can also be deferred until you retire. Remember government savings plans are more about where you deposit the money you want to save. They do nothing to help guide how you should invest. That is, just like a FDIC-insured government savings account, a bank or a similar entity (e.g. Fidelity, Schwab, TD Ameritrade, etc.) that holds the money you deposit will try to steer you (along with various financial advisors) where to invest.

Whether you participate in any of these government sponsored very complex savings schemes depends on a number of variables. It's important for you to understand the most important ones. I hope you will see, given your current age and overall financial profile, you should not participate in most government-controlled savings plans. This may change when you reach 40.

Variable #1 — In most cases, if you withdraw your money from any of these "savings plans" before age 60 (which is at least 30 years from now for the oldest of the four of you) or if you use any of the monies for any need other than their intended purpose, you will pay significant penalties. In most cases, the penalty you pay in the future will negate the benefit of the contribution you make today. In other words, you should have a reasonably high probability you will not need the money you contribute today in the next 30 years. It is unlikely you can come to such a conclusion today.

Variable #2 — You should understand you can defer or eliminate taxes on the investment returns of your personal savings today without the need to restrict yourself to various government controlled savings plans. The easiest way for you to avoid tax on these returns is to invest in a home that appreciates in value, invest in a tax-free municipal bond or shelter your savings in a life insurance policy. The easiest way for you to defer taxes today is to invest your savings in a S&P 500 Index Fund. Moreover, thirty plus years from now, when you withdraw the investment returns from the Index Fund, such returns will be taxed as long term capital gains (in 2015 the maximum federal tax rate for long-term capital gains is 15%) with a reasonable likelihood that such tax rates will be less than the ordinary income tax rates (in 2015 the maximum federal tax rate is 43.4% plus the impact of state and local taxes) required on the IRS savings vehicles. Moreover, you decide when you want to liquidate your money (and pay your tax) since you will not be subject to any IRS minimum distribution requirements.

Variable #3 — In many instances, employer-sponsored government savings programs (e.g. 401(k) plans) incur substantial fees, often times a full percentage point more in annual fees, than fees you would pay if you controlled the investment of your savings. Such charges can often wipe out the primary benefit of the savings that should accrue to you by making deposits with before tax dollars and deferring taxes on your investments until you retire. Remember, you not only pay these fees before you retire, but also during your retirement years when you are still subject to various IRS rules and regulations.

Variable #4 — If you have a negative net worth, that is your debt exceeds your assets, it is unlikely the benefit of deferring taxes on your investment earnings (if any) will exceed the interest cost on today's debt. That is, you would be much better off to avoid any contribution to a government controlled savings vehicle and, instead, use your savings to pay off your debt.

Variable #5 — If your motivation is to receive a tax deduction today for your contribution, then you should have a high degree of confidence your ordinary tax rate at retirement will be lower than the tax rate you pay today. This is unlikely. In the first place, if you follow the road map in this book your wages will continue to increase, hopefully substantially over the next 10 years which will push you into a even higher tax bracket. In addition, given the substantial increase in government debt, it is entirely likely successful U.S. citizens will be subject to higher tax rates in the future, especially on distributions that are taxed as ordinary income.

Variable #6 — Finally, there is no reason to believe the rules which nudge your behavior today will not change, to your detriment, in the future. For example, in early 2015 President Obama proposed to start taxing the popular IRS college tax savings "529" plans. This initiative has since fizzled. However, you should expect similar assaults on tax savings and deferral plans (especially for the more successful higher wage earners) in the future. Look for the Roth IRA and the Roth 401(k) to be future targets.

So, here is my very simple advice for an extremely complex area. If your employer matches your contribution to a employer sponsored government retirement plan (e.g. 401(k); 403(b), etc.), then participate up to the level of the match (which is essentially free money) and invest all of your contributions in a S&P 500 Index Stock Fund. Close your eyes and forget about this investment until age 60. Otherwise do not contribute to any plan that requires a contribution of pretax dollars. However, if you hit the threshold discussed earlier, that is you are rich today and have a reasonably good likelihood you will stay rich between now and age 40, then contribute after tax dollars to a Roth IRA (or Roth 401(K)) and invest these monies in a S&P 500 Index Fund. Once again, close your eyes and hang on until age 60.

If you're interested I can show you the math that supports these relatively simple conclusions. If you continue on your path toward financial independence, at age 40 this advice will change substantially because funding your retirement will now become one of your most important financial goals. After age 40, we will dig deeper into the U.S. extremely complex tax code, which Congress will probably change substantially in the next 10 years. For now, in summary, **stay in control of YOUR money.** Freedom without IRS handcuffs.

INVESTING IN STOCKS

During the next ten years you should avoid investing in stocks until you meet all of the following conditions:

- You have saved one-year of projected annual spending.

- Your career opportunities are excellent and your wages are sustainable and predictable.

- Your house is paid for or you decided to be a lifetime renter.

- You have fully funded future liabilities payable in the next 15 years (e.g. your kids education).

If so, then this indicates either you have received a career windfall (e.g. bonus or lump sum from the exercise of stock options) or you have mastered the art of saving. In any event, you have achieved a certain level of financial success which increases the odds that money you save today can actually sit untouched for at least 15 years. However, a better plan is to assume you won't touch the money you put in savings until retirement (if you're now 40 and plan retirement at 65 — 25 years from now).

A company has two primary ways of financing its capital needs. Debt or Equity. When you invest in stocks, you are investing in the equity of a company. A company that finances 100% of its needs with equity (i.e. it sells shares of equity to shareholders) will also owe 100% of its profits to these same shareholders. As you learned earlier, a company with no debt is often referred to as unleveraged. Therefore, a $100,000 investment in a unleveraged company that distributes $10,000 in profits provides a 10% return to its shareholders.

A company that borrows money to finance its capital needs promises to pay back the principal and interest on its debt before it returns any money to its shareholders. As an additional inducement for a lower interest rate and more favorable principal repayment terms, company founders may personally guarantee the debt and/or provide additional collateral such as a lien on Company assets (buildings and equipment) to its creditors. Therefore, creditors usually can rely on a steady stream of payments from a company. Equity shareholders, on the other hand, only receive a distribution once all company obligations (including payments to all creditors) are made. Over time, in theory, shareholders should receive a higher return compared to a creditor because equity shareholders take greater risk (i.e. less certainty of returns). Because of this risk, equity investment returns over a short period of time can be extremely volatile.

Because of this volatility, once you decide to invest in stocks (equities), there should be a low likelihood you will need to tap these monies before retirement. Time is the only variable that will help you survive market cycles when a large percentage of investment will go poof right before your eyes. During the next decade **the only long-term stock investment you should consider is the S&P 500.** This investment will give you adequate exposure to international and emerging markets as well as the proper mix of large and middle market companies. You don't need greater diversification or more complexity in your long-term equity investment strategy.

The best way to make this investment is to buy a share in a S&P 500 ETF (e.g. SPY symbol also known as Spiders) or a low cost S&P 500 Stock Index Fund. For example, in 2015 the Fidelity Spartan 500 Index Fund charges an annual fee of .05%. Remember, Index Funds are passive investments. That is, once you make the investment, don't touch it, thereby increasing the likelihood that your owner-ship and trading costs are minimal. Reinvest the dividends in the same Index Fund. Close your eyes and hope once you open them in the future that the returns will compen-sate you for taking the risks of an equity shareholder in a company.

What return should you expect over the next 20 or 30 years on your equity investments? Well, not a lot. See, in theory, stocks should be priced based on the value of projected future cash flows (dividends and capital gains) discounted to the present based on an interest rate that reflects the likelihood that the projected cash flows will, in fact, occur. This interest rate (or discount rate) is calculated by adding an appropriate premium to the safest and most risk free securities that exist (U.S. Treasury issues). Therefore, a premium for equity investments reflect the risk and volatility of stock market returns (which, as you know, can generate large losses) relative to more stable returns that have minimal risk.

However, in early 2015, 10-year U.S. Treasuries are yielding approximately 2% (while ten-year government securities in Germany, Japan and Switzerland are yielding almost zero). Denmark, in February 2015, actually cut its interest rate on deposits to a - .75%. In other words, investors in Denmark are actually paying their government a premium (i.e. like insurance) to keep their money safe. Always remember it is today's yield, not past or historical results, that is the best determinate of tomorrow's returns. Consequently, with anemic growth throughout the world you might be fortunate to notch long-term equity annual returns greater than 5%.

Also, keep in mind some simple mathematical truisms when it comes to stocks or other investments. If a stock falls 50%, then it needs to increase 100% in value for you to return to your original investment amount. Similarly, a stock that increases 25% in year one, 50% in year two, and loses 60% in year 3 still has an average annual return of 5%; even though over 3 years it lost 25% of its value. Numbers and statistics can be very deceiving as points of reference to influence your behavior.

Finally, remember the interest payments made to you by creditors are essentially revenue neutral to the U.S. government. That is, you need to pay the tax on the interest expense a company pays to you and the company receives a tax benefit for an equivalent amount of interest. If the overall corporate effective tax rate is equivalent to the individual tax rate on interest received, then the result is identical to a scenario where the corporation would receive no deduction and interest paid to you would be tax free. This is entirely different from how equity is taxed. That is, corporations pay dividends in after tax dollars (i.e. they receive no tax benefit on dividends paid). However, you still need to pay a tax on any dividends you receive from the corporation. Consequently, purely from a federal tax perspective, corporations have a greater incentive to fund their capital structure with debt increasing the overall instability of the entire financial system. That is, unleveraged, anemic long-term equity returns of only 5% do not compensate for the overall systematic risk of corporations that fund their capital needs with debt. The best way for you to potentially insulate yourself from this "hidden" risk is to hold your equity securities for a longer period of time (greater than 25 years).

In summary, Millennials are right to fear the stock market. You've already lived through two periods (2000 and 2008) where the stock market experienced significant losses. Your only benefit is you have time on your side; but only if you take advantage of it.

Always keep in mind short-term trading in individual stocks is actually speculating (it is not investing) and therefore should be reserved for monies allocated from your entertainment budget. The Stock Market Game (spoon-fed to high school and junior high school students) is nothing more than a promotional gimmick sponsored by the leading trade group for the brokerage industry. Play Monopoly or Risk instead; you will learn more. **Buying stocks without an in-depth knowledge and insight of a company's operations, business risks and overall financial condition is a fool's journey.** Even professional stock traders recognize they need to exceed the market returns by at least 2% a year to absorb the management fees and costs to trade. Individuals have even a higher performance threshold because their lack of scale increases both trading costs and the opportunity cost of their time.

OTHER INVESTMENTS

There are literally thousands of investment products that others might encourage you to participate in during the next 10 years. Mutual funds that invest in emerging market debt and stocks. Hedge funds that invest in currencies, commodities, futures and other derivatives. Individuals who want you to buy gold, silver, diamonds, and colored emeralds. Funds that invest in tobacco bonds, Puerto Rico debt and the State of Illinois. Venture capitalists who pitch various deals in technology, green energy and biotech. Master limited partnerships that operate energy pipelines, rail systems and other infrastructure.

Financial advisors will work hard to convince you markets don't necessarily price these investments efficiently and therefore there is a tremendous opportunity to those with the courage to act expeditiously. Maybe. However, the more likely scenario is that speculators are chasing unsustainable returns as they become more and more complacent about risk. These asset bubbles will eventually burst and there is a reasonable likelihood you will feel the pain of the sudden collapse if you follow their advice.

My advice. Run quickly from these nut cases and their exotic ventures and securities. If there are opportunities, it is unlikely these shady individuals (probably with credit scores below 600) are going to find them. Trust me, there is a lot more that will go wrong with these wealth creating ideas than what will go right. Moreover, always remember financial advisors and active investment managers are essentially nothing more than professional gamblers who saddle you with 100% of their losses, while capturing a perpetual income annuity made up of fees and trading commissions.

Also, as a relatively small investor you are going to feel more and more of a pull to invest in crowdfunding activities of friends, family and others. Most of these start-up companies will fail, which is why financial advisors advocate a spray and pray investment philosophy. **Put your shotgun away, load up on cash and keep your powder dry.** Time is on your side and the benefit or patience is more valuable than waste from haste. Opportunities will always be around the corner. In 10 years, when you develop the vision of a sniper, you will be in much better position to identify the winners of tomorrow.

Despite these constraints, there are a couple of investments I want you keep on your radar during the next 10 years. The first, which I mentioned earlier, is real estate. Use K.I.T.E. to educate yourself in the various nuances of real estate investing. Read books on real estate, listen to active investors, understand the various investment models and even invest a small amount of money in some publicly traded real estate investment trusts (REITs).

The second is collecting. There are literally hundreds of different things you can collect (e.g. coins, stamps, art, antiques, guns, comic books, chess sets, wine, etc.). Your goal, however, would be to move beyond a passive hobby of collecting to an active passion of investing. Collecting is a niche market and therefore it takes many years to become an expert. However, only as an expert can you minimize the likelihood that you are duped by counterfeits and/or you overpay for an item. You will learn many nuances of successful investing. For example, you will better understand why scarcity impacts value. You will see how to enhance (or restore) value of things that others have written off as worthless. You will appreciate that when you buy you prefer minimal competition and yet when you sell, well, competition is what increases value for things that are rare.

Although illiquid, collecting does pay dividends in the form of pure enjoyment plus it occasionally provides a certain amount of social hipness. Most collectibles will trade with minimal transparency and therefore price discovery is often difficult. Nevertheless, despite such constraints, collecting, like real estate, provides you a tangible asset that stays under your control. It may ultimately be more satisfying than loaning your money to governments, banks and hedge funds for safe keeping. However, like most investments, you need to approach this asset class with extreme caution.

YOUR BIGGEST INVESTMENT — YOUR KIDS

In 2004 Gerry McIlroy made a $350 legal wager with 500-1 odds that his son, Rory would win the British Open golf tournament in the next ten years. In July 2014 Rory did indeed win the tournament by two strokes. Gerry's investment on his son returned $175,000.

Perhaps it would be nice if all of us could write an option on the day our kids were born with a return that would reflect the odds of achieving certain milestones in life. Would such an incentive increase the likelihood all of us would be better parents? If we knew today our son or daughter might be a potential lottery ticket (e.g. Lebron, Tiger, Serena, etc.) might it motivate all of us a bit more? Boy, I hope not!

However, that said, if you choose to have kids one of your biggest decisions will be how much you want the help of science. The field of genetics is increasing exponentially. It is no longer a question whether you can design your offspring, but whether you will. Do you pass on your genetic code, and that of your child's mother, the old fashioned way? Or, do you screen for certain biological markers and remove those variants that increase the risk of certain diseases and keep those that have traits you value. Since your offspring will compete in the future with a global population of genetically designed adults, this will make your decision increasingly difficult. A mathematical algorithm cannot predict your children's destiny. Genes matter, but how you nurture your children will still have a tremendous impact on their success.

I always felt the **money we spent on you was an expense**, but the **time we spent with you was an investment.** Sadly, many parents believe the opposite. That is, the more money they spend on their kids, the larger the return on their investment. Especially with young athletes, some parents are spending thousands of dollars on coaches, trainers, and psychologists. However, as they push for a return on their investment, they may be increasing the chances of an unfavorable outcome.

If we invested our time right, then there was a very high likelihood the return we would feel from watching you succeed would be our reward. On the other hand, if we made a poor investment with respect to the quality and quantity of our time, then we ran the risk of increasing the financial costs to ourselves, or to society, in the future. It was for this reason, after I turned 45 in 2001 (with Mom's urging and support), that I totally reprioritized my tasks so I could spend more time with each of you. I was lucky. All of you were still relatively young and thus was the benefit, at least to us, of waiting to have children until our careers were well on their way to successful outcomes.

However, that said, the actual cost to raise a child will be one of the single largest financial obligations in your lifetime. How much? Well, if you take this responsibility seriously, the cost to raise a child, EXCLUDING college education, could easily exceed $300,000 (in today's dollars). The amount pays for food, shelter, healthcare, transportation, and other basic necessities. In the unlikely event your child has special needs, this amount could easily double. If you average $50,000 a year for thirty years, this investment could easily exceed 20% of your lifetime earnings. It's a difficult task and the outcome is anything but certain.

If you have children, especially more than one, they will represent your largest investment of your savings and your personal time. Children are a choice, and like other preferences require trade-offs. You and your spouse will shoulder most of the financial burden of raising the next generation of responsible adults. It is an awesome duty with the primary reward being the pure joy of seeing your kids blossom in the same manner that your mother and I have witnessed your evolution.

The quality of your kid's childhood is 100% your responsibility, which you hopefully will share with an equally responsible spouse. If you don't want cigarettes, alcohol, drugs, Internet (including Porn and other unsavory websites), overly violent video games and other addictions to poison their development, you must proactively monitor their behaviors and shape their environment with your values. Genes will always explain a large portion of human variation in both physical and mental capabilities, but the way you nurture the development of your children, especially their early life experiences, will have a tremendous impact on how they develop. If they are damaged because of your neglect it will not only negatively impact your life, but sadly and more importantly, the life of your kids.

This will take a significant amount of your personal time (your non-working hours). That is, if you follow a 3:3:3 time investment; one-third of your time sleeping; one-third working and one-third personal, then your personal time per week will be 56 hours. During your kids non-college years no less than one-fourth of this amount; a mere 14 hours a week should be devoted exclusively to family time; that is, on average 2 hours a day. Clearly if you have a spouse who shares child rearing responsibilities this will be a tremendous benefit to your children. To raise your kids with the greatest opportunity for success requires a significant sacrifice of time that you could be spending pursuing other activities. That is, your children will reap a greater return on the personal time you invest interacting with them versus the financial dollars you spend on them. Remember, the hope of your children are invested in you!

To summarize, my advice would be if you and your spouse don't want to devote the resources, especially your time, to raising children, then don't have any. Both you, and the children who would have suffered because of your lack of attention, will benefit.

MANAGING RISKS

UNDERSTANDING
THE VARIABLES YOU
MUST CONTROL TO BUILD
A SUSTAINABLE MODEL
FOR TOMORROW

Every choice you make involves some element of risk. While the elements each of you use to evaluate risk may be different, the process necessary to make an informed decision is strikingly similar among most individuals. If you are going to make better decisions, then you must understand this process. I call this process E.C.O. consciousness, or being E.C.O. conscious. E.C.O. is another acronym which emphasizes the importance of your personal Experiences, your current state Condition and the Outcomes you anticipate. It essentially incorporates the elements of past, present and future.

Experiences	→	Past
Condition	→	Present state
Outcomes	→	Future state

The past is essentially your life's experiences or how you assess the experience of others, all of which continually evolve right up to the point you actually make a decision. Condition reflects your present state of mind especially when it comes to a snapshot of your financial affairs. As I mentioned earlier, almost every decision you make has some form of immediate or future financial impact. Betting the house means different things to different people. What might be a material gain or loss to you may be immaterial to others. Outcomes refers to your future state position after all uncertainties with respect to your decision are known. Your ability to assess this future state outcome at the time you make your decision is usually what determines whether you made a "right" or "wrong" decision. Decision making is a skill, and like all skills, the more you embrace the elements of Knowledge, Insight and Technique, along with Experience (K.I.T.E.), the more likely your decisions will achieve your desired outcomes.

Responsible people can make decisions that have bad outcomes and reckless people can make decisions that often seem to turn out okay. However, many adverse consequences occur because individuals lack the experience to make the decision, their present state of mind is impaired (reflecting irrational hope or despair) and/or they poorly assess the variables that impact the outcome of their actions. Preferences, behaviors and emotional state will often be the catalysts that cause people to be blind to many risks.

Increase the time between the decision and the outcome and you increase the percentage of variables that are unknown or unknowable.

Time is the most important variable when it comes to assessing the probability of achieving a future outcome.

Certainty of outcome is higher for an outcome that may reveal itself in the next five minutes versus an outcome that may not be known for the next five years. The greater the time between decision and outcome the more important it is to build contingencies and options for adverse alternatives.

You must think through the possible consequences of your choices, both short- and long-term. Rational people make irrational decisions because they don't consider the consequences (both in a narrow and broad context). Many who do consider the outcomes overestimate the benefit and understate the cost.

In addition, many decisions require you to opt in to or opt out of a particular action. In other words, every decision you make reflects something you choose to do or something you choose not to do. The only difference is sometimes it's not possible to know the outcomes of decisions you choose not to make. I don't know what my life would have been like if I started my career at KPMG versus EY. What I do know is that it would be vastly different.

To achieve financial independence you must be able to see risks that others don't identify or recognize. Instead of the entrepreneur who is overly optimistic with respect to a particular opportunity, you might actually achieve better outcomes by being the risk arbitrager. That is, you understand the difference between risks that offer a high likelihood of positive rewards versus those risks that offer a high probability of negative outcomes. For example, now is the time to take the risks in your current career; not risks in long-term investments.

Your ability to see future state scenarios in a bit more clarity than those around you will have a tremendous positive impact on your success if you learn how to incorporate this clarity into your daily decisions making. Some like to call this intuition; I like to say you are being E.C.O. conscious.

To achieve a high level of E.C.O. consciousness you need to develop and sustain a certain lifestyle. Some of you have already achieved several lifestyle milestones. My objective in the following paragraphs is to remind you and your peers the importance of these milestones and discuss other lifestyle choices you need to consider during the next decade. How you choose to incorporate these choices into your daily life will impact how you assess your present state condition when it comes to future decisions.

AVOID THE POVERTY ANCHORS

Congratulations! Two of you have already avoided life's greatest poverty anchors and the youngest is well on his way to achieving a similar outcome. As you might recall, most of these anchors manifest themselves before age 25. You did just the opposite. Finish high school. Check.

College educated with tangible skills. Check. No marriage before developing a clear career path. Check. No kids. Check. No kids before being happily married. Check. Married an independent college-educated professional spouse. Check.

Not surprisingly, research continues to demonstrate what most of us would consider common sense. Married households of highly educated professionals (usually college educated; but not necessarily) who begin their families after they have successfully initiated their careers tend to be better off financially, and therefore are more likely to build savings for emergencies and future opportunities. My hope, for you and your children, is that you avoid the complex web of stepchildren, divorced spouses (and their families), child-support payments, and family visits that require you to stay glued to a particular geographic location. Dysfunctional families are the biggest poverty anchors that derail professional careers and destine many of their children to a similar mess.

ALIGN LIFESTYLE CHOICES WITH YOUR CAREER

As you progress through your 30s, it will be important to pause occasionally and assess whether your major lifestyle choices are consistent with your career objectives. There are several factors that impact this assessment; however, typically the ones with the greatest influence are where you live, your family, your health, your savings, and specifically the relationship between the time you invest in work versus the time you invest in other activities.

REPLACING PEDS WITH PELS

You earn luck but don't help a fickle fate. Your health is your most important asset. Good health drives productivity. Monitor your health including key metrics like blood pressure and cholesterol. Eat right and exercise. Fruits and vegetables, little fat, less salt, easy on the sugars, and go easy on the alcohol. Stay away from processed foods. Minimize the fast food and the chips, cookies and ice cream that populate the shopping carts of the obese. Exercise. Weigh yourself every day. A healthy weight is the most important metric that will help you avoid life's most preventable and devastating illnesses. Know the source of the food you eat and the supplements you take. Understand the deferred liability of sickness is hidden in the poisons and toxins that populate our food supply. Finally, make sure you get enough sleep.

If you pursue a performance-based career you are going to feel significant pressure to use performance enhancing drugs (PEDs). PEDs can be prescription based (Adderall and Ritalin) or in form of numerous supplements that are not approved by the Food and Drug Administration. I have no ethical bias against smart drugs. However, read the science and understand the side affects. More and more scientific studies are challenging whether the drugs actually deliver on their promises.

Your goal should be to replace PEDs with a Performance Enhancement Lifestyle (PELs). Learn to optimize what you eat, how you exercise, when you sleep and include a proper mix of healthy relationships. If you successfully manage a healthy lifestyle you will minimize the cause of many diseases and the need to add ingredients that might prove to be toxic when used over a long period of time. Adjust your lifestyle rather than always turning to medications. A PEL (not a pill) is often the best way to feel good each day and perform at your highest level.

FIND AN EXERCISE ROUTINE

Exercise, for many people is pure drudgery. There are numerous reasons for this. Sometimes it reflects the endless conflicts between one's professional and personal lives. Often an individual is so far out of shape that they are too tired to start a new exercise routine. Occasionally a person might have some type of physical ailment they will use to rationalize their lack of mobility. Maybe they have already decided prescription drugs (or illegal substances) are a better way to treat anxiety, attention deficit disorder, insomnia and other mental disorders. However, in almost all cases, the reasons most people don't exercise in their 30s is because there is no immediate consequence to their poor lifestyle decision. The one thing these couch potatoes will learn is the longer they go without making exercise a lifestyle priority the greater the likelihood they will have miserable health outcomes in the future.

You will minimize this risk if you find a sport or exercise activity you actually enjoy. If you find an activity you can enjoy for many years, well, all the better.

I've participated in many exercise routines over the years, but as you know from earlier in this book, the sport I have played consistently since my early 20s is racquetball. I love racquetball. Maybe it's because in a period of an hour of vigorous activity on a 800 square foot court I can travel between 4 and 5 miles. Perhaps it because the violence of propelling a ball to a speed that exceeds 100 miles an hour actually has a calming effect on my demeanor (I'm always less irritable after a good game). I certainly enjoy the mix of stamina and skill. There's an inner peace that allows me to forget, for a short period of time, whatever stress might be waiting for me when play is over.

Performance still drives me so I always play to win but I've learned to enjoy the game even if I lose. I'm a better player today than I was in my 20s only because K.I.T.E. helps to guarantee I'm always in a process of continual learning. When you compete (against yourself, a clock or an opponent) you are always looking for the optimal mix of speed, strength and mental capabilities. That's what makes it interesting, because whether in sport or in life there is always someone that performs at a slightly higher level. There is always something to work on that will help you get better, even if the constraints increase with age.

However, unlike your career, competition isn't necessary for you to receive the very real benefits of exercise. In your lifetime I'm convinced science will continue to confirm what most of us who exercise already understand — there is a verified link between exercise and the pleasure neurotransmitters serotonin and dopamine. Moreover, a lot of my most creative thinking (including ideas for this book) occurs when my mind is left to wander during exercise. How can you resist something that makes you more happy and less fragile? So leave the digital world that seems to consume all of us. Hop on your bike, put on your hiking boots, slip on your running shoes, and lace up your boxing gloves. All of you have a great start in this effort. Keep it up. In many ways it doesn't matter if you compete in a sport, work out at the gym or take a walk once and awhile through the woods. Remember, the more you enjoy what you are doing the less you think about the activity and the more you will actually embrace the pure joy that comes from exercise.

ANXIETY, STRESS AND OTHER MEDICAL AND PHYSICAL BARRIERS TO PERFORMANCE

It was late fall 1958, my mother was busy in the kitchen frying french fries and making dinner for our family. Like most two-year-olds, I was pretty rambunctious. I ventured into the kitchen, reached up to the counter, and promptly pulled a cup of hot grease over my head. Personally I don't remember the actual event. I guess shock does that to you. With my skin peeling off of my head, face, neck and chest my parents grabbed me and rushed off to the emergency room at the local hospital.

I spent the next several months in burn therapy, my head wrapped in gauze that was changed multiple times during the day. Over time, the burns began to heal. Not surprising, my parents always had a difficult time revisiting the horrors of that day, but I learned later how fortunate I was (relatively speaking) that our family physician had developed a particular skill in treating burns during his tenure as a physician during World War II. As I slowly came out of the fog that erased my memories of this terrible accident and its aftermath, it became increasingly apparent to my parents that the robust vocabulary I had developed as a two and half year old had vanished. In its place was a bunch of mumbled sounds that were indecipherable.

For the next twelve years, through the eighth grade, I was in extensive speech therapy. I probably should have stayed in therapy longer, but I was tired of the daily taunting by other kids, the lack of inclusion in certain classes because I wasn't "normal," and the perception by many adults that the inability to pronounce a variety of words and to articulate long phrases was a sign of stupidity.

Moreover, this midwestern born boy had developed a bit of an East Coast twang primarily because my early speech teacher hailed from Boston.

I think my parents had come to the realization that the cost of keeping me in speech therapy was quickly exceeding the benefits. Of course it didn't help that I had recently gone through puberty and the subtle scars on my neck were now increasingly apparent any day that I did not shave multiple times. Just to make matters worse, playing any type of competitive youth sports was a challenge because spending my first nine years living in a small apartment was not the ideal environment to develop any reasonable coordination. I was a mess.

Still, I was lucky because I had what others could only wish for. I had great parents who constantly pushed and pulled me forward with words of encouragement and processes of inclusion that made me feel I could smash through most barriers with hard work. I had siblings and friends who often shielded me, or defended me, from the poisonous comments of arrogant insolent peers. I had a caring spouse, extended family and other adults who helped me overcome numerous anxieties. In other words, I was nurtured in an environment that was focused on my success and well-being.

All of you, and everyone you meet, is fighting, or will be fighting, certain demons and a dark- ness in their lives. There are no perfect humans. Scars might be physical or emotional. They might be genetic or they might arise from a tragic accident or other unfortunate trauma in one's life. Everyone is fighting something that prevents them from performing at their highest level. The difference is high performance people have learned ways to mitigate their weaknesses, manage their weaknesses and/or turn them into strengths. **High performers don't make excuses.** They play the cards they are dealt in the most advantageous way possible.

Without question, my deficiencies made me more competitive and had other overriding benefits. The physical scar on the left side of my neck made me more comfortable sitting at the head of the table, or at the far left of all of the participants at any particular event. It was funny in a way, I would prefer making eye-contact with as many people as possible because it made me feel they weren't staring at the scar on the side of my face. When I did presentations, I was always over prepared, had everything well rehearsed and had responses ready to almost any conceivable question. I just had no desire to stumble over my words and relive the sneers from my childhood. I even scripted my phone conversations early in my professional career. Although I was never as polished as some of the more impromptu conversational speakers, I did learn to present with a certain sincerity that made it easier for people to trust me. Perhaps, more importantly, I had a certain compassion for those less fortunate, especially those who have this uncanny desire to fight their disabilities in the hope they can be better and function more effectively.

Environments shape all of us. I was probably born an extrovert and then morphed into an introvert because of the events in my early childhood. **Everyone is morphing into something. Sometimes it makes us different, other times it makes us better and sadly, it often makes us worse.** In this digital age, how your environment shapes you becomes increasingly important as background checks, group interviews and various tests for skills, drugs and personalities become the new barriers to even the most basic entry level positions of high performance jobs. **Image** is important and it **needs to be developed and managed like any skill.**

As discussed earlier, masking physical pains or mental issues with opiates, stimulants, supplements, anxiety drugs or other medications that have a high propensity for dependency may not be the best path to sustain long-term performance. Stress is an ongoing part of life. The more you learn to manage it with a natural healthy lifestyle (nutrition, exercise, sleep, meditation and other mindfulness training), the greater the likelihood you will stay in better control of outcomes while minimizing adverse side effects.

All of you have demonstrated the ability to battle through certain prejudices and stereotypes. It's important you continue to do so in the future, regardless of what fate bestows upon you. The better you become in this effort, the more your positive approach to life can help lift others from the darkness of their despair.

TAKE RESPONSIBILITY FOR YOUR HEALTH

As you might remember, it was right before Christmas in 2013 that your Grandma entered the hospital with difficulty breathing and other symptoms of chronic heart failure. Although my Mom was only 78 years old, and a 15-year survivor of breast cancer, recent ailments had been taking their toll for almost a year.

Mom grew up during a period where physicians were pillars of their community. Mom's primary care physician had overseen her care for almost 40 years. Both my mother and my father, put tremendous trust in his advice and counsel. There was almost a paternalistic approach to the way he practiced medicine.

Around Thanksgiving 2013, as Mom got progressively worse, I decided to take a proactive approach to managing Mom's care. Sadly, health care had changed over the last 40 years, and not for the better. Her one doctor now seemed detached as Mom spent time with five specialists in multiple different practices. There was no one coordinating her care. Each specialist would order endless, and often times overlapping diagnostic tests, and the results would be buried for months in each specialty's self-contained medical records. When she entered the hospital, Mom was on a cocktail of 15 different medications, each with their own side effects, and no one had any insight on how the mixture was actually helping Mom get better.

It was Christmas Eve when the on-duty physician pulled me aside and told me Mom was dying. It broke my heart. It was too late for my Type A, hands-on personality to make a difference and on December 29, 2013, my Mom came home to Hospice. I managed the Hospice process with Mom until she died in the early morning of April 16, 2014. The Hospice nurses were great, but on the one occasion I had to meet with the Hospice physician, the same detached, out-of-touch persona came flashing back.

I don't know what happened to the medical profession during the past 40 years. Maybe it was as simple as Mom's primary care physician turning 70 and taking a longer time than normal to transition to retirement. Perhaps physicians feel like nothing other than pawns in the labyrinthian bureaucratic supply chain among insurance companies, hospitals and various government entities. I guess it is possible they are upset HMOs and similar organizations now manage patient care, because their profession has shown some were inept at doing it themselves. Since they don't have time to spend with patients, I suppose it's easier to prescribe a pill than to actually proactively manage a long-term chronic disease. Or, it could be their incomes are being squeezed by escalating malpractice premiums and lower payments for their services. What started out as a heroic profession for many, is now nothing but a charade for those who have spent too many years fighting the bureaucratization of medicine.

Although statistically it is unlikely in the next ten years you will be a significant consumer of health care resources, you need to recognize this changing environment. If you continue to eat right, exercise and manage stress there is a pretty good chance you may not even have a need to see a physician during this time period. However, if you do, there are three critical things you must do.

First, you must understand the key healthcare metrics that describe your health today and might influence it in the future. Your healthcare data files need to be as important as your financial files (perhaps even more so). It's important you understand the results of any diagnostic procedures. You should have access to the raw data of your genome and you should consider proactively identifying your genetic risks so you can manage the ones you can. You should be constantly aware of false positives and false negatives, and seek second independent opinions especially for any high risk procedures. You should never be in a position where a new physician or other healthcare worker, prior to any recent diagnostic procedure, knows more about your health than you do.

Second, identify and communicate with a healthcare advocate. Your healthcare advocate should be someone you trust explicitly. It might be your spouse, a significant other, a brother, or Mom or myself. The number of physicians are decreasing as the needs of the population are increasing. You cannot rely on anyone with a vested interest in the healthcare delivery system to work in your best interests. You and your advocate must work in your best interests. Your advocate is a sounding board. Depending on the care you need, you may want them to participate in physician meetings just to listen to what is being said and to help you think through logical questions during what might be a very emotional process.

Third, research your physicians and your healthcare networks. Healthcare is like any other profession today. There are excellent providers and then there are numerous shoddy operators. Be careful. The more critical the procedure, the more important the quality of the physician and his network. Never trust your physician implicitly (just like other professionals or advisors). Be proactive. Do your research. Always ask about alternatives and trade-offs.

In addition, if children are in your future you should do everything you can to give them the greatest opportunity for success. If you participate in the biological process, then you and your spouse (or significant other) must take care of yourself if you expect your children to be born healthy. Plus, like it or not, designer babies will be, if not in your future, part of your children's future. Whether eliminating a defect responsible for a serious disease or enhancing an offspring's physical characteristics or intellectual capability, genetic engineering of early embryonic cells has arrived. Nurture is critical; but nature, for many families, will be left less to chance. How you participate in this process may be one of your greatest challenges.

In closing, please recognize you are responsible for your health and the health of your children. Do not trust any bureaucracy, corporate or government, with your care (or those you love). Keep your insurance intact with a private carrier and consider the benefit of private "concierge" physician groups; which you will see proliferate in the next ten years.

MARRIAGE, INFIDELITY AND DIVORCE

One of the most important decisions you will make during your lifetime is whether you should marry and who you should marry. A great lifetime partner will significantly increase your chance for career success and your family's overall happiness. However, if you choose the wrong partner, or if the marriage fails for other reasons, then your path to financial freedom will become much bumpier.

If you marry, have children, and then decide to divorce, this will further complicate your future financial picture and potentially create life-altering scenarios for your children. In most scenarios, when you divorce, you share joint custody of your children. **When your children spend 50% of their life in an environment you don't control, you lose a tremendous amount of input into shaping their behavior.** This lack of influence will have a significant impact on the moral and ethical underpinnings that drive their decision making. The environment that does shape their behavior will most likely not be as positive as the one you would have created for them if you were able to stay happily married to a spouse who shared your values.

There are many variables that impact a healthy marriage. However, one of the biggest causes for divorce, the likely outcome from an unhealthy marriage, is infidelity. You need to understand this risk and how to minimize it.

As a man, there is a greater likelihood you will cheat on your spouse purely because of testosterone. That is, men who tend to cheat on their spouses do so because they are dissatisfied or tempted sexually. Women, on the hand, usually cheat because they are emotionally dissatisfied. What's sometimes interesting, however, is men actually are more upset if their wife has an affair because they are dissatisfied sexually while women are more upset if their husband has an affair because they are emotionally dissatisfied.

Environment impacts many of our decisions and such things as working one on one with others, spending late nights at work and traveling frequently without your mate increases the likelihood you may cheat on your spouse. Sadly, if you are unhappy in your relationship then cheating on your spouse actually doesn't help. It will just make you unhappier. The best way of course to minimize infidelity and the likelihood of divorce is to have a marriage where both partners are happy and are satisfied with their lives. If both parties develop excellent relationship skills then there is a greater likelihood conflicts can be resolved through healthy communication. Marriage takes work. If you work together to have a satisfied relationship, both of you will have a significant competitive advantage in your march toward financial freedom.

CHARACTER AND REPUTATION

Whew, you're almost done. I'm going to close *Getting to 40* with an expanded topic that appeared in the beginning of *Getting to 30*. It is the

Protect your name and reputation at ALL cost.

topic that poses the greatest risk to your career over the next 10 years and that is how you build your character and manage your reputation. It is one of the most difficult topics to write about because the world does not function within the ethical and moral boundaries that were part of your upbringing.

Character reflects those qualities unique to you and reputation reflects how others see you.

Some people you meet are not ethical, too many are out and out dishonest. Incentives, or the lack of incentives, will persuade them to lie to achieve their desired outcomes. These outcomes will almost always focus on their own personal or financial self interests. Seldom will they even consider what might be best for you or others you care about.

This section will not discuss or try to analyze why people behave the way they do. **Human behavior is complex and there are a myriad of reasons why people behave the way they do. However, the environment of nature and nurture (past, present and future) will always be the most critical variable in understanding human behavior.**

Individuals, especially those who lack resources, will use every excuse possible to rationalize illegal behavior. Elites, on the other hand, will use their power to weave conflicts of interest, promote nepotism, and reward self dealing to convince all of us their unethical behavior falls within the boundaries of existing laws. Just remember, once you start down the slippery slope of ethical and moral degradation, it's very difficult to reverse course.

As you know, there are several models that identify different types of personality profiles. However, I've never been exposed to any models that do a good job assessing a person's character. Therefore, I've developed my own model which basically assigns people to four basic categories that describe their character which is the harbinger to their reputation. Theses four categories are as follows:

Integrious
Corrupt
Opportunistic
Naïve

INTEGRIOUS

Integrious people adhere to a moral or ethical code of conduct. They are relatively steadfast in their core beliefs but they are open minded to the views of others. They can be aggressive in taking advantage of opportunities but they seldom take advantage of others. Integrious people are competitive but they believe in fair play and a level playing field. They prize honesty in their relationships. They may not be religious but they follow the Golden Rule when dealing with others. They have the humility to face up to their mistakes. They loath manipulation. They have a high level of self esteem and are not easily intimidated by those who have different values or beliefs. They have courage to stand up for what they believe is right, especially to those in authority. Often they are the only voice for what others think but are afraid to say.

Integrious people seek wisdom so they can become wise.

You seldom read much about Integrious people (in fact, it is not even considered a word in most dictionaries) because only a small percentage of humans fall into this category and their deeds are not, in general, promoted among broad communities. However, sometimes they are the easiest to identify. Integrious people are the good listeners. They work hard to seek truth because they understand how easy it is to manipulate and distort wisdom.

Unfortunately integrious people tend to be followers and not leaders. As such, you often see them mopping up the messes of more unsavory individuals. All communities need to find better ways to identify integrious individuals and help them develop the appropriate leadership skills.

Integrious people usually have strong personalities; but they can become weak when they start to believe others behave the way they do. They obey the rules; others don't. They tell the truth; others lie. They check the boxes of integrity and then become oblivious to the risks. In fact, integrious people so much want to believe others are good that they often cross over to the land of the Naïve.

You should strive to be an integrious person and an icon that others want to emulate. This is not easy, especially in today's fragile world; one that is peppered with land mines that are easily tripped with relatively minor miscues. When news (whether true or not) travels quickly, through the endless postings that make up our social and professional networks, it becomes increasingly difficult to manage the daily risks that might question your character and destroy your reputation. Moreover, apps like Memo, Yik Yak, and Whisper now allow anyone to post anonymous messages about friends, peers, bosses, employers and numerous other relationships. **It's important to take risks, but "mistakes" in today's digital world will not be forgotten.**

Minor indiscretions can easily explode into major embarrassments. As a result, your reputation is constantly being shaped in today's digital world through a constant barrage of memos, emails, photos, text messages, posts, tweets, etc. Often it is the stress of this daily popularity contest that causes many integrious people to give into the temptation of others or to quit fighting for what they believe is right; what they believe is true. **Integrious leaders must learn how to build and manage their identity in the wired world of the internet.** This might be one of your most important steps in shaping how others view you and your values.

CORRUPT

Corrupt people adhere to no moral or ethical code of conduct and therefore they are the polar opposite of integrious people. Their acronym for character is C.O.I.N. **Corrupt people actively solicit the opportunistic, cautiously avoid the integrious and aggressively prey on the naive.** They are blatantly dishonest and they know it. They aggressively create opportunities that further their own or their constituents self interests, without any regard to the consequences it might have on others.

A week's worth of local, national and international headlines ring with sounds of corruption: Stanford Probes Claims of Cheating; Brazil Cracks Open Vast Bribery Scandal; Cow's Milk Found in Breast Milk Sold Online; Atlanta Educators Lose in Cheating Trial; Oil Giant to Pay Big Fine for Illegal Iran Work; Wylys Hit With Big Sanctions on Fraud; Former Virginia Governor Gets Two Years; Port Scandal Spawns Suits; Corruption Charges Fly Over Helicopter Deal; Brazil Charges Bribery in Embraer Sale; Lab's CEO Quits Amid Probe; Ex-SAC Trader Gets Nine-Year Prison Term; Workers Say Train Repairs Were Often Bogus; Lloyds Settles Rate-Rig Probe; Fraternity Chapter Closed After Video of Racist Chant.

Corrupt activities always occur outside the boundaries of established policies (rules, laws and regulations) and almost always involve a conspiracy among multiple individuals working together to accomplish a variety of self interests. It usually involves elites that are politically or economically powerful and therefore believe policies don't apply to them. However, it also includes leaders who are not part of the main stream and work in the vast underworld of various (and often quite numerous criminal enterprises). Corrupt individuals prize lack of transparency and accountability. The more opaque the transactions, the better.

Small acts of illicit activity are often the nexus for broader corrupt behavior. All of us are involved in various forms of illicit activities. We violate rules, disobey laws and/or participate in a morally unacceptable behavior. Usually people who are involved in an illicit activity do so knowingly (cheating on one's taxes, participating in an extramarital affair). However, knowledge is not a prerequisite for one to perform an illicit activity. Many people unknowingly break rules because they are not aware of a rule, law or policy (which, as you know, can vary greatly among communities). In addition, individuals can also be morally complicit and yet not be criminally culpable. For example, adultery might be a moral failure and yet it is not a crime (at least in the United States).

Most illicit activities are relatively benign (exceeding the speed limit or lying about your golf score) or not tremendously malevolent. Basically, we are all sinners. However, **when your illicit or other activities begin to harm others then you have joined the world of the corrupt.**

Corrupt activities can be blatantly obvious (drug cartels and other criminal enterprises) or subtle (trading sex for political favors). In almost all situations there is some form of cronyism whereby elites provide money, jobs or favors in exchange for support. Corruption schemes can vary but generally they include crooked businessmen, villainous politicians and doyens of the dark markets acting in concert in patterns similar to the following:

1. A small group of executives give a green light to a specific project.
2. The bidders for the project are identified by the executives.

3. The executives and the bidders conspire to select the winning bid.
4. The executives overcharge the winning bidder an agreed upon amount.
5. The bidders funnel the excess charges to various shell companies.
6. The shell companies make kickback payments to all of the elites involved in the process (the executives, the bidders and/or politicians or regulators).

Corrupt people learn how to weave inappropriate behavior into the seams of a community's culture until the lawlessness it breeds becomes acceptable policy. Clearly, you don't ever want to be corrupt or part of a corrupt organization.

Both performance-based and activity-based workers can be involved in corrupt activities. For example, it is the PB worker that bribes the AB employee in order to streamline a complex regulatory process that requires numerous permits and approvals. In addition, individuals trapped in an activity-based job or a low-paying performance-based job often have the urge to cross over to the shadow, dark or black markets. It is unlikely you would be pulled into such a career path. However, many hard-working low-skilled AB or minimally skilled PB workers become prized PB employees in criminal networks that value the skills of money laundering, extortion, kidnapping and racketeering. Such jobs might also include numerous illegal services such as sex workers, drug dealers, gun traffickers, etc. Many people who want to work and are unable to find well-paying jobs find this is the best way to maximize the value of their output. Sometimes individuals who can't see the light of opportunity in the legal economy will seek illicit income in the darkness that cloaks the shadow markets of the underworld.

OPPORTUNISTIC

Opportunistic people push the moral, ethical and legal boundaries of their communities. They operate in the gray zone between the integrious and corrupt, usually pushing the boundary that is closer to corruption.

Opportunistic people know the rules and **learn how to exploit policies** (rules, laws and regulations) **to achieve maximum advantage for themselves and their constituents.** This exploitation can either be in the form of using policies to impede others or identifying loopholes that accelerate their own objectives. Fuzzy interpretations, subjectivity, and confusion usually work to their advantage. Opportunistic people thrive on ambiguity. In other words, what they do is a very conscious and calculated act. They are clever; but seldom wise.

If they break a rule, they do so because they have gone through at least an informal process that rationalizes the benefits of breaking the rules exceed the costs (including the probability) of being caught. **Opportunistic people do not confuse the ethical with the legal.** That is, if it's legal, then it's ethical. Opportunistic people know how to capitalize on the gray that separates black from white.

Opportunistic people learn the fine art of trading favors for money (political donations today for tomorrow's ambassadorships, cabinet positions and State Department advisory positions). Hiring well connected individuals (often friends and family members) into coveted executive positions in exchange for future business transactions or other forms of loyalty. They understand the value of cozy relationships between the regulators and the regulated. There are never any conflicts of interest unless there is a specific rule that states a particular relationship or transaction is illegal. Perhaps most importantly, **opportunistic**

individuals know if you control the environment, you control the outcomes.

Iowans are opportunistic when they can convince regulators to turn half of the state's corn into ethanol. China is opportunistic when they hold down the value of their currency to promote trade as they export deflation to the rest of the world. The New England Patriots are opportunistic when they deflate footballs for a competitive advantage.

Trump and Hillary are opportunistic. They understand how relationships and their networks provide access to the people who control the forces of R~I~P~P~L~E~S. As opportunists they know the relationships they build during their time as politicians can easily be monetized after they serve their terms in office (through paid speeches, serving on corporate boards, providing private consulting services, etc.). In contrast, corrupt politicians actually monetize their value while they are in office (through bribes, kickbacks, conflicts of interest, etc.).

People who are opportunistic never lie; they tell falsehoods. They never cheat; it's called gamesmanship. They don't bribe; they tip. They don't extort; they incentivize. They don't pay kickbacks; they give gifts. They never have errors in judgement (but the people who they relied on for advice might); they have transgressions. They avoid talking about corruption and instead focus on others "mismanagement."

Opportunistic people operate in the murky interface between legal and lawless. They seldom ever apologize for their actions because in their minds they never did anything wrong.

Within the boundaries of your own personal ethics and morality you must be opportunistic if you are going to increase your likelihood of success during the next decade. However, you need to recognize there is a very fine line between activities that are corrupt and those which are opportunistic. You should favor the other boundary. That is, become an **Integrious Opportunist**. Like any skill, K.I.T.E is your best tool to develop an opportunistic mindset within appropriate boundaries that preserves your integrity. Remember, ICON with no I spells CON.

NAÏVE

Naïve people lack K.I.T.E. (Knowledge, Insight, Technique or Experience). Often they don't know what they don't know. Most of the time they are pawns being adeptly positioned in a game they don't know they are playing. Naïve individuals certainly can be simpletons (uneducated, unstable and fragile). Moreover, they may lack a moral compass or a clear understanding of a community's culture or policies. However, many times they are extremely successful in one particular domain which often leads to a level of overconfidence in areas where they have minimal knowledge. Individuals who are corrupt and opportunistic exploit people who are naïve. Ignorance is never bliss when you are being manipulated by others.

The best way not to be naïve is to be skeptical.

Naïve people are more likely to unknowingly aid or participate in the commission of crimes or other activities that border on the immoral or unethical. They tend to be followers and usually don't question the decisions of others.

As you now know, my first professional job trained me as a skeptic. The greatest problem-solving skill of a skeptic is the ability to reason and think critically. Critical thinking is what allows one to distinguish the quality of evidence in building an argument and to express conviction and support for conclusions that are inconsistent with fraudulent representations. All con artists look for those individuals enamored with their own personal confirmation biases (older adults or senior citizens) or those who show a lack of ability to identify logical fallacies (the innocence of youth). Then, like a magician, the con artists manipulate us, and sadly, only with the pain of hindsight do we recognize how easily we were tricked.

Skeptical people always pursue K.I.T.E., especially in areas where they recognize their lack of background might light the fuse that becomes the bomb of reckless decisions. Not surprising, educated people who embrace continuous learning are less likely to be nudged into behaviors that are not in their best interests or fall outside their ethical and moral boundaries.

There is always more to learn. If you assume you know it all, then you only impede what you know. When K.I.T.E no longer matters it is only a matter of time before others will exploit your ignorance.

Trust, but verify, was a consistent mantra I followed early in my career. Later in life, the mantra morphed into verify, then trust. You must follow a similar mantra, especially when it comes to decisions or transactions that could have significant adverse personal or financial consequences if you are wrong. Checks and balances exist in all enterprises for a reason. You should develop similar controls with respect to your daily decisions.

CLOSING COMMENTS: CHARACTER, REPUTATION AND LEADERSHIP

I hope some of the suggestions below will help you navigate what has become very treacherous terrain. **The best way to develop strong character and a stellar reputation is to become a "great" leader.**

First, recognize how you lead. There are literally thousands of techniques to get people to behave the way you want to achieve the outcomes you believe are important. However, many of these techniques rely on various forms of manipulation, coercion, extortion and other forms of unethical behavior. You want people to respect your authority but you might be surprised how their performance improves if you take a sincere interest in mentoring their success. Every leader I ever respected had a certain amount of personal integrity and consistent principles that helped them recognize the difference between vice and virtue.

Second, understand how you follow. Leaders look for patterns of behavior and consistency of performance. They want individuals they can depend on, especially in the most difficult of situations. They want people who keep commitments and meet deadlines. They want workers they can trust and confide in. They want people who can lead others. They want professionals who will help make them more successful. There is nothing wrong with being a good follower of a great leader. However, **great leadership qualities are ubiquitous in all facets of life.** The more you understand these qualities and the more you develop these traits yourself, the more likely those you choose to follow will deserve your loyalty and you (and others) will benefit from their wisdom.

Third, be careful who mentors you. There is a very dark side to human nature. Bad mentors have a way of convincing you what is wrong is right because everyone does it, we've always done it that way, this way is more fair, there is no rule against it, we won't get caught, etc. In other words, the outcome always justifies the means. Unscrupulous mentors have a way of convincing you it is okay to cut corners, take shortcuts, accept kickbacks, bribe, steal, lie, embellish, cheat and perform other forms of unsavory and even illegal acts for the sole purpose of gaining some type of competitive advantage; either for yourself, for your mentor or for your employer.

Always remember corrupt leaders are very good at insulating themselves from illegal and immoral acts while allowing their underlings to take the fall for their misdeeds. Never forget many "leaders" standing on pedestals are often nothing more than sly swindlers with sweet tongues who are the pundits of dishonor. Their hope is you will be the one who eventually will bear their scarlet letter.

Leaders recognize that greed and self interest drives the behaviors that determine outcomes. We constantly move along a continuum that is bounded on the extremes by altruistic and narcissistic activities. The most ethical companies, like EY (and there are many others) adopt formal codes of conduct and develop appropriate internal controls to combat conflicts of interest and other natural tendencies of human nature. They understand the importance of setting and enforcing boundaries with respect to behavior. Such companies and organizations value and perpetuate a culture of integrity, virtue and honesty. The best way to insulate yourself from professional risk to your reputation is to align yourself with such organizations.

Strive to understand the specific metrics that drive performance or the lack of incentives that might impact behavior. If you find yourself in an organization where you believe the metrics and incentives reward the wrong behavior, then become the leader who changes the metrics, changes the incentives or implements the controls that balance the natural human tendency to behave badly. Don't rationalize the pursuit of corrupt and unethical endeavors. Change the policies and change the culture. Aspire to something greater than the dark side of human behavior. Seek the obvious truths. Be the hidden gem. Recognize that often what is legal is not ethical and many times inconsistent with the spirit of a community's policies and rules. If you cannot change the culture, then better to leave an environment where you might become engulfed in an entity's corrupt endeavors.

In today's environment reputation is based on professional talent and personal character. Great performers can quickly become the poster boys for bad behavior (Alex Rodriguez, Ray Rice, Tiger Woods, and Bill Cosby) and suffer significant adverse financial consequences for their lack of judgment. Your goal is to avoid such notoriety. Don't be the pariah who tarnishes tomorrow's headlines with the infamous quote of contrition, "I stand before you as a heartbroken and humble man." **Recognize your personal code of conduct is the cement that holds together the sometimes fragile virtue of your personal integrity.**

Money will always flow to those who have the ability to control resources, shape infrastructure, decide policy, control prices, appoint leaders and regulate education. You live in a world where politicians are adept at extracting favors from the system, private interests co-opt the system and citizens cheat the system. Sadly, this is the environment you need to be aware of and function in on a daily basis.

Everyday you will be presented with decisions that will test your character and most of these decisions will not have a clear black or white response. Should you disclose a relationship where you personally benefit from a transaction where others might believe you have a conflict of interest? Shouldn't the substance of a transaction be more important than the form? Should you participate in retrograde behavior because there is no law against it? Won't we see the killing and suffering of animals for our pleasure as barbaric in the future? There are no easy answers to many of the decisions you make.

Understand your personal weaknesses and **stay away from environments that might tarnish you.** Avoid situations in which your self control might fail. Make decisions that minimize your exposure to temptations. Recognize that individuals who have a high level of self control are those who actually stay away from the more seedy surroundings, rather than those individuals who believe they can overcome such environments and the related distractions. Don't forget being in the wrong place at the wrong time (whether or not you participate in any illicit activities) will give your adversaries sufficient ammunition to make your life miserable.

EPILOGUE

BE THE 1%

Money will always be a difficult topic to write about because of a natural association with greed and corruption. However, not talking about it is not going to make such issues go away. My view is the more you understand its value and how to use it to achieve harmony in your life, money becomes an asset and not a liability. Therefore, I write because I know what awaits your own lives when it comes to money and the financial challenges it creates. I'm confident the major themes you read in today's headlines will not change in the next twenty plus years. Moreover, even though I am a data point of only one, I do believe the principles in *Getting to 30* and *Getting to 40* will survive not only your lifetime but many generations.

I mentioned in the Prologue that the five principles discussed herein essentially boil down to a circle of success with the icons of Earn, Consume, Save, Invest and Give. Visualize for a moment a ring on your finger that would glow different colors as you move through life. Earn; Green, Consume; Red, Save; White; Invest; Yellow and Give; Blue. When you start college the rings shines a fire shade of yellow and red. As you enter your career the tint shows more green with hints of white as you expand your horizons. The hope of course is eventually the ring begins to show a bright shade of sky blue as you recognize your success now, more than ever, allows you to transition into the role of Giver, a topic for later discussion in Getting to 50 and beyond.

I hope R-I-P-P-L-E-S provides you the foundation to better understand how macro and micro environments impact a community's standard of living. Every decision has an economic consequence that benefits or harms someone and every leader needs a source of money to fund their most mission critical initiatives. The more you understand the actual source of this money, the better you will be at reconciling the economic agenda with the moral, philosophical or ideological principles articulated by a leader. If you disagree with the agenda of others, frame your criticism cautiously. Often there are no easy answers when trade-offs require a negative impact on some community.

At age 40, you will be **R~I~P~P~L~E~S.** You will be a **R**esource others will depend on; so take care of your health (physically and mentally). The environment where you choose to work, live and play will provide you the **In**frastructure that will be key to your success and happiness. The **P**olicies you choose to support will define your character. What you earn will demonstrate how others **P**rice the value you contribute to your community (but not your value to the community). As a **L**eader you will be the anchor that others look to for guidance as they sail through their stormy lives. **E**ducation and learning will define your skills and reflect your wisdom. As uncertainty reins around you **S**tability will reflect the calmness of a lifestyle that you know is in balance.

I want you to focus on your career and to better understand how to identify, develop and optimize the skills that will increase the likelihood you are compensated for the value you deliver to the workplace. Never be ashamed to price yourself high and let others ratchet down your expectations. Over the long run, how you build your career will be the most important variable in how you will live in retirement. All of you are well positioned to take advantage of the exploding digital revolution that will reshape core industries of education, healthcare, energy, and entertainment using artificial intelligence, personal health monitoring and other processes. Who knows what today's drones, robots, 3D printers and smartwatches will give way to in the future. Just merging your three career interests in sports, the brain and design presents fascinating possibilities.

My goal has never been to raise you as an investor. Sure I understand investing might be necessary to prevent inflation from eating away at your savings. However, I think it's more important during your 30s to build a career that increases your savings and to develop spending patterns that embrace a deflationary mindset. In any event, you can't become an investor until you're a saver, and at age 30 you are still a long way from accomplishing this objective. If you develop a successful career, coupled with controlled spending, then it will be easier to have success as an investor. Why? Because the risks you will take will be more rational, increasing the likelihood the returns you realize will fairly compensate you for such efforts.

I can't overstate the importance of learning how to save; not just for your personal benefit but also for the benefit of society. Today, more than ever, you need to develop a greater cushion to protect you from tomorrow's unknowns. No debt, cash reserves, and minimal fixed monthly expenses are your best defense against future contingencies. This is the best way for you to build immunity from the risk of losing a job, unforeseen health issues, future educational needs, unexpected expenses and other unanticipated events. It will give you the greatest flexibility to bounce back from some of life's most severe crises.

Saving, of course, means you must consume less than you produce. However, the paradox of thrift also means sometimes you need to spend more today in order to consume less tomorrow.

Your decisions do make a difference, no matter how small. In most cases it will not be in your benefit to follow the herd. The herd will always borrow and spend in the hope their contribution to growth will protect them from the consequences of their decisions.

I want you to be rich now that you understand what it means to be rich. Rich doesn't mean you have lots of money. Rich means you have developed a lifestyle where you don't need to worry about money. As you can better appreciate, the guiding principles to achieve wealth (focusing on your career, learning to save and managing your risks) are not the same as the strategy to sustain wealth (invest with wisdom). I hope this book helps you build that model. A truly flexible model that helps you rebound from bad events. Blending your career skills with a certain amount of financial savvy will help get you there. *Getting to 30* and *Getting to 40*, as you probably now recognize, is nothing more the story of how we became "rich." Our values and traditions are our legacy and your inheritance.

Luck will always manifest itself in a single event. However, chasing outliers will not increase the probability of success. True excellence exists only if it is able to be sustained over long periods of time. Instead of certainties think in terms of probabilities. Failure is no prize when you make bad decisions. Learn from your mistakes but more importantly learn from the mistakes of others. Liquidity (having sufficient cash reserves) is your biggest friend during periods of uncertainty. Wisdom is what you seek. It's healthy to keep an open mind and change it when you have new knowledge and insights. In the long run, a life long pursuit of learning is what will separate you from others and make you exceptional.

Keep an open mind by seeking knowledge and insight from sources that disagree with you who will often come from different backgrounds and socioeconomic strata. Daily you will see the ugliness that permeates the human race. However, search for the good and the inspiration that comes from it. Stay optimistic and try not to become a cynic.

We are proud of all of you. There is no greater reward than the joys of being a parent to your sons or daughters. Each of you have unique skills and therefore different career paths will help you explore and see the world from varying perspectives. There are many different paths to success and sometimes the road less traveled provides the greatest happiness. Remember, your differences are your strengths. All of you have so much potential to make a positive impact on your families and the world. In many ways, your journey is just beginning. Be true to yourself. Take care of yourself and each other.

Embrace your relationships as brothers, your current and future relationships with your spouse, and with your children. Those relationships are the ones that bind us. Those family relationships are second to none. Embrace those relationships; relationships others wish for, dream of and seek in the darkness of their despair. Those close family relationships, along with the deep and trusting relationships you forge with friends and other family members, will serve you well in the future.

There's a certain grace I hope you follow throughout life. Winning is important but a certain etiquette that values sportsmanship is still a worthwhile endeavor. Mom and I hope all of you will continue to be: hard-working; respectful; humble; grateful; responsible; giving; caring; successful; of strong character and ultimately happy. In other words, a nice mix of grit, swagger and humility. The journey can be hard but joyful. As you turn 40, life's purpose for you will become clearer and I have no doubt you be ready to change the world, if that is your desire. In any event, I hope you will have the financial flexibility to pursue your dreams, whatever they might be. As you will learn, happiness without worrying about money is the true Agile Advantage. If you accomplish this objective and hold onto your character, reputation and a certain humbleness, well, welcome to the 1%.

Love, Dad (and Mom)

GETTING TO 40
ACKNOWLEGMENTS

It was the summer of 2009. I was with my youngest son Brandon, enjoying lunch at a quaint outdoor cafe outside of St. Peter's Basilica in Rome, Italy, when our conversation turned to world affairs. It was during one of our spirited exchanges that the idea of using Ripples as an acronym to explain economics started to crystalize. Originally, Ripples was going to be a stand alone book, but the years passed, my sons grew older and *Getting to 40* was now a priority. So, I condensed Ripples and wove it in as a major theme in *Getting to 40*.

If you haven't noticed already, Brandon did all of the design work. The cover artwork, the layout, the graphs and the cool Geib ambigram. I'm forever grateful for his efforts but much more appreciative of the results. Somehow he found a way to squeeze this project in over the 2015 summer while working a full time job at the Cleveland Zoo. While Brandon worked on the design I enjoyed vibrant content conversations with Benjamin, who has a constructive way of challenging and making me think about almost everything that I write. Grant and his wife Stephanie (a most pleasant addition to our family) are anxiously waiting to read the finished product as they aggressively and successfully continue to pursue their career goals. In the background, of course, is Monica, my wife of thirty-two years, who did much of the editing, proofing and questioning some of my more thought provoking conclusions. Hugs and kisses to all of you.

There are a number of other family members and friends (colleagues from Ernst & Young, classmates from

270

The University of Chicago and others) who took time to read various drafts and provide their comments and insights. Thank you. Unnamed but not forgotten.

Finally, a special shout-out to the team at MoneyThink in Chicago. Greg, Ted, Kristen, Jennifer and others. A team of Millennials helping the youth of America achieve financial independence. The net proceeds from the sale of *Getting to 40* will go to MoneyThink to help them accomplish their mission. I urge others to support them in this endeavor.

ABOUT THE AUTHOR
DOUGLAS G. GEIB II

Douglas G. Geib II is CEO of Geib Investments, Inc. He is a former Corporate Finance Partner and a former Audit Partner with Ernst & Young LLP and a former Board Member, Senior Executive Vice President and Chief Financial Officer of FirstCom Inc. In October 1999 FirstCom was Bloomberg's #1 fastest growing publicly traded technology company in the United States. FirstCom built state of the art fiber optic networks in Chile, Colombia and Peru.

Mr. Geib has a Bachelor of Science and Business Administration (BSBA) degree from The Ohio State University, graduating summa cum laude and a Master of Business Administration (MBA) with honors from The University of Chicago. He is a licensed Certified Public Accountant (CPA).

Doug, who is 59 years old, lives in Ohio with his wife Monica and their beloved dog Reese. The author can be contacted at douggeib@mac.com.

CPSIA information can be obtained
at www.ICGtesting.com
Printed in the USA
FFOW04n0104190915
16891FF